Religion

Editor: Danielle Lobban

Volume 458

independence
educational publishers

First published by
Independence Educational Publishers
The Studio, High Green
Great Shelford
Cambridge CB22 5EG
England

ISBN-13: 978 1 86168 918 4

Printed in Great Britain

Printed and bound by the Pureprint Group using it's environmental print technology, a low-carbon, low-waste independently audited process that reduces environmental impact using 100% renewable energy, vegetable-oil-based inks and no industrial alcohol. 98% of all dry waste and 95% of press cleaning solvents are recycled. Pureprint are ISO 14001, EMAS and FSC certified and holds the Queen's Award for Enterprise: Sustainable Development.

FSC www.fsc.org MIX Paper | Supporting responsible forestry FSC® C022913

Acknowledgements

The publisher is grateful for permission to reproduce the material in this book. While every care has been taken to trace and acknowledge copyright, the publisher tenders its apology for any accidental infringement or where copyright has proved untraceable. The publisher would be pleased to come to a suitable arrangement in any such case with the rightful owner.

The material reproduced in **issues** books is provided as an educational resource only. The views, opinions and information contained within reprinted material in **issues** books do not necessarily represent those of Independence Educational Publishers and its employees.

Although every effort has been made to ensure that website addresses are correct at time of going to press, Independence Educational Publishers cannot be held responsible for the content of any website mentioned in this book.

Images

Cover image courtesy of iStock. All other images courtesy of Freepik, Pixabay, Pexels, and Unsplash.

Additional acknowledgements

With thanks to the Independence team: Janey Hills, Klaudia Sommer and Jackie Staines.

Danielle Lobban

Cambridge, May 2025

Contents

Chapter 1: Understanding Religion

Chapter 2: World Religions

Chapter 3: Religion in the UK

Introduction

Religion is volume 458 in the **issues** series. The aim of the series is to offer current, diverse information about important issues in our world, from a UK perspective.

About *Religion*

What is religion, and why do people follow it? This book explores major world religions, their beliefs, and practices. Discover what faiths have in common, how religion shapes society, and its role in the UK today. A guide to understanding religion with respect.

Our sources

Titles in the **issues** series are designed to function as educational resource books, providing a balanced overview of a specific subject.

The information in our books is comprised of facts, articles and opinions from many different sources, including:

- Newspaper reports and opinion pieces
- Website factsheets
- Magazine and journal articles
- Statistics and surveys
- Government reports
- Literature from special interest groups.

A note on critical evaluation

Because the information reprinted here is from a number of different sources, readers should bear in mind the origin of the text and whether the source is likely to have a particular bias when presenting information (or when conducting their research). It is hoped that, as you read about the many aspects of the issues explored in this book, you will critically evaluate the information presented.

It is important that you decide whether you are being presented with facts or opinions. Does the writer give a biased or unbiased report? If an opinion is being expressed, do you agree with the writer? Is there potential bias to the 'facts' or statistics behind an article?

Activities

Throughout this book, you will find a selection of assignments and activities designed to help you engage with the articles you have been reading and to explore your own opinions. Some tasks will take longer than others and there is a mixture of design, writing and research-based activities that you can complete alone or in a group.

Further research

At the end of each article we have listed its source and a website that you can visit if you would like to conduct your own research. Please remember to critically evaluate any sources that you consult and consider whether the information you are viewing is accurate and unbiased.

Issues Online

The **issues** series of books is complemented by our online resource, Issues Online.

On the Issues Online website you will find a wealth of information, covering over 75 topics, to support the PSHE and RSE curriculum.

Why Issues Online?

Researching a topic? Issues Online is the best place to start for...

Librarians

Issues Online is an essential tool for librarians: feel confident you are signposting safe, reliable, user-friendly online resources to students and teaching staff alike. We provide multi-user concurrent access, so no waiting around for another student to finish with a resource. Issues Online also provides FREE downloadable posters for your shelf/wall/table displays.

Teachers

Issues Online is an ideal resource for lesson planning, inspiring lively debate in class, and setting lessons and homework tasks.

Our accessible, engaging content helps deepen students' knowledge, promotes critical thinking, and develops independent learning skills.

Issues Online saves precious preparation time. We wade through the wealth of material on the internet to filter the best quality, most relevant and up-to-date information you need to start exploring a topic.

Our carefully selected, balanced content presents an overview and insight into each topic from a variety of sources and viewpoints.

Students

Issues Online is designed to support your studies in a broad range of topics, particularly social issues relevant to young people today.

There are thousands of articles, statistics and infographs instantly available to help you with homework, research, and assignments.

With 24/7 access using the powerful Algolia search system, you can find relevant information quickly, easily and safely anytime from your laptop, tablet or smartphone, in class or at home.

Visit issuesonline.co.uk to find out more!

Chapter 1

Understanding Religion

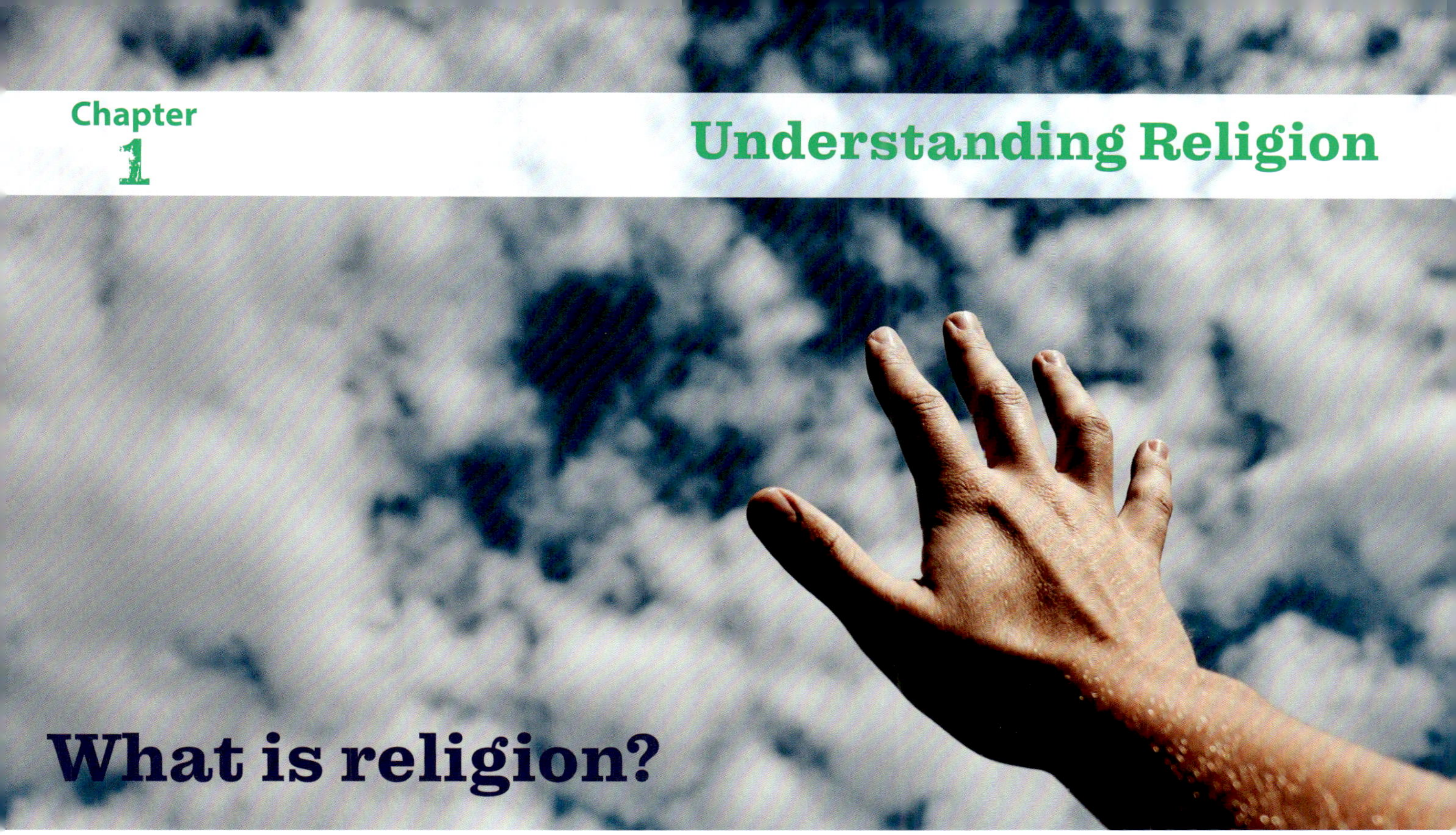

What is religion?

Have you ever wondered why some people pray, celebrate certain holidays, or follow special rules about food and clothing? These actions are often part of a religion – something that has shaped lives, communities, and cultures all over the world for thousands of years. But what exactly is religion, and why do so many people follow one?

What is religion?

Religion is a set of beliefs that helps people make sense of life. These beliefs are often about how the world began, what our purpose is, and what happens after we die. Many religions believe in one God or many gods, while others focus more on nature, ancestors, or spiritual ideas.

Most religions have their own stories, symbols, and ways of worshipping. People might gather in a church, mosque, temple, or synagogue to pray together. They may follow a holy book, like the *Bible*, *Qur'an*, *Torah*, or *Vedas*, and live by certain rules or traditions. For some, religion is something they practise every day. For others, it may only be part of special times in the year. And some people don't follow any religion at all – which is also completely okay.

Why do people follow religion?

People follow religion for many different reasons. Some are born into religious families and grow up learning certain beliefs and traditions. Others choose a religion later in life because it feels right for them.

Religion can offer comfort during hard times. It can also help people feel connected – to a community, to their history, or to something bigger than themselves. Many people say their religion gives them strength, hope, and guidance. It can teach people how to treat others with kindness, honesty, and respect.

How many religions are there?

There are thousands of religions in the world. Some of the largest are Christianity, Islam, Hinduism, Buddhism, Sikhism, and Judaism. Each one has different beliefs, festivals, and ways of worship. But many religions also share similar values – like caring for others, telling the truth, and being grateful.

Even within the same religion, people may have different traditions depending on where they live or what their family believes. That means there isn't just one "right" way to be religious.

Religion in everyday life

You can often see religion in everyday life. People might wear religious symbols, eat (or avoid) certain foods, or take part in religious festivals. Think of Ramadan, Diwali, Christmas, Hanukkah, or Vaisakhi – all important times in different religions.

Religion can also inspire music, art, clothing, and even laws in some countries. Whether or not you follow a religion, you've probably come across its influence in some way.

A final thought

Religion means different things to different people. For some, it's at the centre of their lives. For others, it's not something they connect with at all. What matters most is that we respect each other's choices and beliefs. Learning about religion can help us understand the world better – and understand each other too.

5 main world religions and their basic beliefs

By Mary Gormandy White, M.A.

While there are thousands of different religions in the world, the five oldest religions are generally described as the main world religions. These religions are Buddhism, Christianity, Hinduism, Islam, and Judaism. Discover some basic facts about these religions and get an overview of their core beliefs.

Population percentages by religion

The followers of the five main religions make up a significant majority of the world's population. The faiths considered to be the "big five" world religions are the oldest ones but not necessarily the ones with the most followers. They are generally considered to be the most widely recognised and influential religions. Close to three-quarters of the world's population practices one of the five main religions. Population percentages by religious affiliation break out as follows:

Religion	Population Percentage
Christianity	31.5%
Islam	23.2%
Hinduism	15%
Buddhism	7.1%
Judaism	0.2%
No religious affiliation	16.3%
other religions	6.7%

Christianity overview

Christianity is the largest religion in the world, with more than 2 billion believers worldwide. The United States is home to the largest Christian population, but Christianity is widespread in many other places, including Canada, Mexico, the Philippines, several African nations, many European countries, and numerous Caribbean islands. There are many versions of Christianity, including Catholicism and various protestant denominations, each differing in many ways yet remaining similar in central teachings.

- Christianity is a monotheistic religion, which means that followers believe there is only one true God.
- Worship of God is an important aspect of Christianity.
- Christians believe in the Holy Trinity, represented by the divinity of the Father (God), son (Jesus) and the Holy Spirit.
- Christian teachings are grounded in the *Old Testament* and the *New Testament* that together form the *Holy Bible*. There are several editions of the Christian *Bible*; not all denominations use the same version.
- Christians believe that Jesus Christ is the son of God, sent to earth as a man and a messiah to save people from their sins.
- A central focus of this religion is the belief that Jesus died as a result of being crucified on a cross, leading to the forgiveness of mankind's sins.
- After being entombed for three days, Jesus rose from the dead and then ascended from Earth to heaven to be reunited with God.
- Christians have faith that there will be a second coming in which Jesus will return to Earth and take Christian believers back to heaven with him.
- The Ten Commandments play an important role in Christian teachings.

Islam overview

Islam is the second largest religion in the world, with an estimated 1.8 billion followers. Muslim is the term for people who follow the Islamic religion. This religion is believed to have begun in the 7th century BC in what is now Saudi Arabia. While Muslims live in many countries worldwide, they make up the majority of the population in several countries. There are seven countries where more than 90% of the population is Muslim (Algeria, Bangladesh, Egypt, Iran, Iraq, Turkey, and Pakistan). Some places follow Islamic (Sharia) law. Key facts about Islam include:

- The Islamic faith is monotheistic, believing in Allah as the one true God.
- Islamic places of worship are referred to as mosques.

Five main world religions

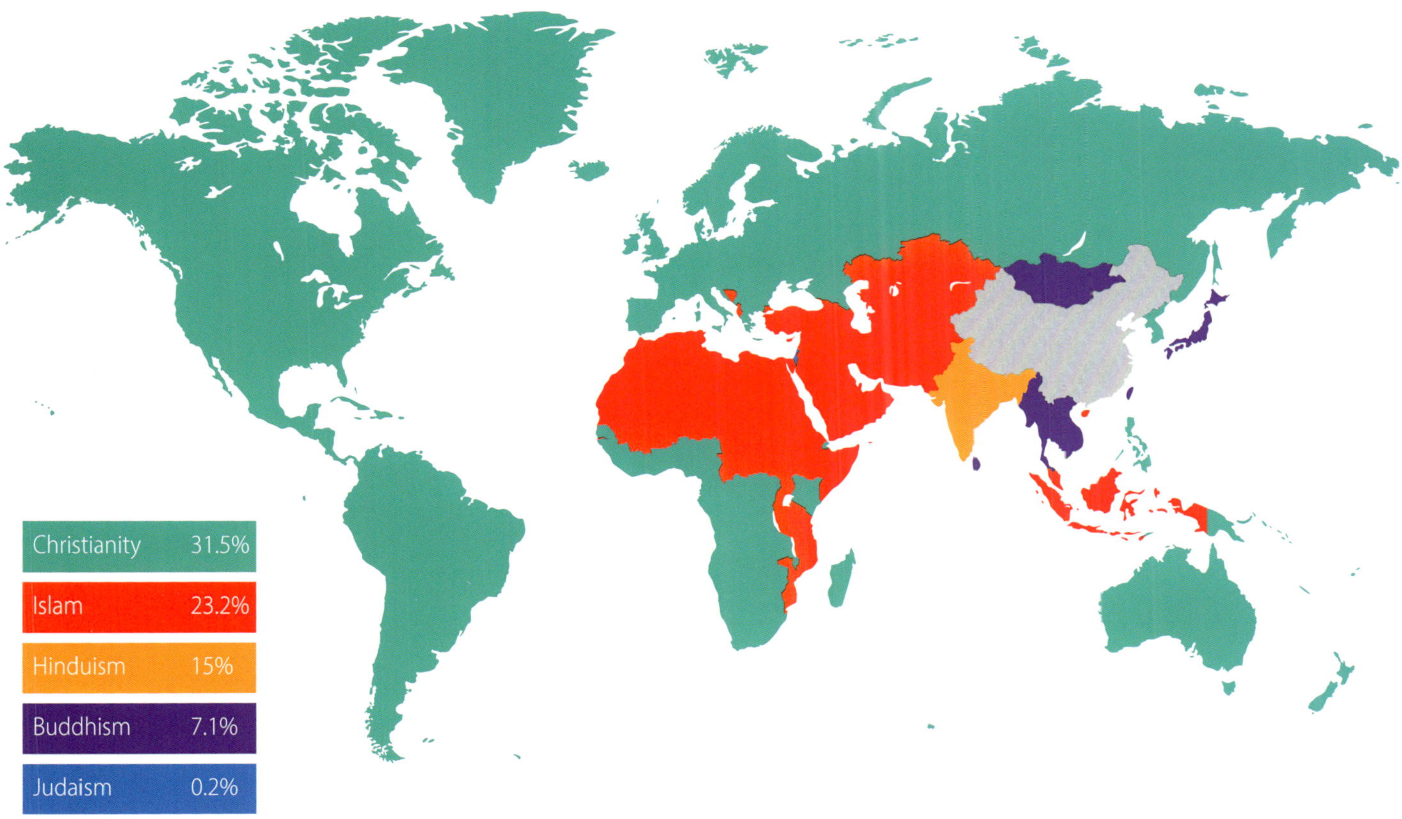

- Those who follow Islam commit to living life in submission to the will of Allah.
- The Islamic faith teaches that the prophet Muhammad is Allah's final messenger, who continued to receive messages from Allah to share with the people.
- After Muhammad's death, other leaders rose in his place under a system called the caliphate, with the individual leaders being referred to as caliphs.
- There are two major sects within Islam: Sunnis and Shiites. The majority (90%) of Muslims are Sunnis.
- Muslims pray at five specific times throughout each day, following a specific prayer ritual.
- Followers of Islam are required to fast during the month of Ramadan.
- Muslims are expected to complete a pilgrimage to the holy city of Mecca at least once in their lives.
- Many Muslim women wear a hijab that covers their hair, while others wear a niquab or burka, which conceals more of their appearance.
- The *Qur'an* is the holy book of Islam.

Hinduism Overview

Hinduism began in India around 2300 BC and remains prevalent on that subcontinent. As of 2018, about 94% of those who follow the Hindu faith live in India. It is third largest religion in the world, with fewer followers than only Christianity and Islam. As with all religions, there are multiple sects of Hinduism, each with some variations in their practices. Core beliefs of Hinduism include:

- Hinduism teaches that God's presence exists in all of creation.
- In the Hindu faith, God goes by many names and manifests in infinite ways.
- Brahman is the recognised supreme deity (God) responsible for creating everything in the universe. Brahaman has no gender and is all-knowing and all-present.
- Shiva and Vishnu are the other primary Hindu deities (gods).
- There are many other deities (called devis), demi-gods (called devas) and goddesses, with significant variations among specific sects.
- The divine essence (called atman) dwells within each person.
- Hindus believe in reincarnation, with a constant cycle of being born, living and dying on the path to enlightenment.
- A person's karma, which refers to the net of their good and bad deeds in the last life, determines the level into which they'll be reborn.
- Rather than a single religious book, Hinduism has a number of sacred texts, including the *Vedas*, the *Samhitas*, the *Upanishads*, the *Ramayana*, and the *Bhagavad Gita*.
- Yoga practice is an integral component of Hinduism.
- Cows are viewed as sacred in the Hindu faith; eating beef is prohibited.

Buddhism overview

Buddhism was founded in the 5th century BC by Siddhartha Gautama, who later became known as the Buddha. After giving up an extravagant life of excess, the man who came to be known as the Buddha discovered enlightenment through giving up his wealth and position to live a simple life as a monk. His efforts to teach others how to do the same became the foundation of Buddhism.

The vast majority of Buddhists live in the eastern and southeastern regions of Asia. There are numerous traditions within Buddhism, each with varying practices. Theism is not fundamental to Buddhism, though it is part of some Buddhist traditions. Fundamental beliefs of Buddhism include:

- The primary focus of Buddhism is to seek enlightenment.
- The Buddha is not worshiped as a god. He was a man and is recognised by Buddhists as such.
- The foundation of Buddhism is based on a set of three universal truths and four noble principles.
- Consistent with philosophy's principles and truths, Buddhists follow a path of moral living, thinking and behaviour, as well as seeking wisdom.
- Buddhism has five precepts to which followers are expected to adhere. These precepts dictate that Buddhists refrain from killing, stealing, lying, misusing sex, and using drugs or alcohol.
- Karma is an important factor in Buddhism, focusing on each individual's responsibility and accountability for their own actions.
- Buddhists believe in reincarnation and rebirth. In the Buddhist tradition, being reincarnated means coming back as yourself multiple times, while rebirth involves returning as an entirely different entity.
- The Buddhist religion includes a number of sacred writings, in the form of scriptures and texts, that share the Buddha's philosophy and teachings.

Judaism overview

Judaism is the smallest of the top five religions. The worldwide population of Jewish people is estimated to be approximately 14 million. About 41% of the Jewish population lives in Israel and 41% lives in the United States, with the majority of the remainder concentrated in Europe and elsewhere in North America. There are multiple denominations of Judaism, including Orthodox, Conservative and Reform. Core teachings and practices of the faith include:

- Judaism is a monotheistic religion, with followers recognising and worshiping only one true God. It is actually the oldest monotheistic religion.
- The Ten Commandments play an important role in the teachings of Judaism.
- Even beyond God's law outlined in the Ten Commandments, righteousness and justice are central to the teachings of Judaism.
- Israel is an important place in the hearts and minds of the Jewish people, both for its historical significance in relation to their faith and its designation as the promised land in the *Bible*.
- The Hebrew *Bible*, which is also referred to as the *Tanakh*, is the primary holy text of the Jewish faith. It includes the same books as the *Old Testament* of the Christian *Bible*, though they are in a different order. The first five books of the Hebrew *Bible* form the *Torah*.
- The *Talmud* is another holy text in Judaism. It includes an extensive collection of Jewish laws and various teachings specific to the faith.
- Synagogue is the name for Jewish houses of worship.
- Young people in the Jewish faith go through Bar Mitzvah (boys) and Bat Mitzvah (girls) ceremonies to symbolise that they have reached adulthood in terms of their responsibilities to the faith.

15 most widely practiced religions

While the five oldest religions, as detailed above, are generally considered to be the five main world religions, they are certainly not the only ones. Some newer religions are among the most popular faiths, defined as those religions that are most widely practiced worldwide.

1. Christianity (2.1 billion)
2. Islam (1.3 billion)
3. Hinduism (900 million)
4. Chinese traditional religion (394 million)
5. Buddhism (376 million)
6. Primal-indigenous (300 million)
7. African traditional and Diasporic (100 million)
8. Sikhism (23 million)
9. Juche (19 million)
10. Spiritism (15 million)
11. Judaism (14 million)
12. Bahai (7 million)
13. Jainism (4.2 million)
14. Shinto (4 million)
15. Cao Dai (4 million)

11 May 2021

Timeline of religion

Ancient religions

c. 4000 BCE
Earliest Egyptian myths recorded

c. 3500 BCE
First written evidence of religion in the world recorded on Sumerian tablets

2300 BCE
The Rigveda begins to form in India – an early root of Hinduism

2000 BCE
Early forms of Judaism emerge among Semitic tribes

Classical religions

1500 BCE
Vedic religion develops in India, forming the base of Hinduism

Sikhism was founded by Guru Nanak in Northern India

1200–1000 BCE
Traditional dating of the Exodus, an important event in Judaism

600–500 BCE
Zoroastrianism arises in Persia, centred on the god Ahura Mazda

563–483 BCE
Life of Siddhartha Gautama (the Buddha) – Buddhism is founded

599 BCE
Life of Mahavira, founder of Jainism

6th century BCE
Confucianism and Taoism develop in China, influenced by Confucius and Laozi

1st century CE
Christianity emerges from Judaism in Roman-occupied Judea

Religion in the Common Era

4th century CE
Christianity becomes the official religion of the Roman Empire

610 CE
Prophet Muhammad receives the first revelation – Islam begins

1054 CE
The Great Schism divides Christianity into Roman Catholicism and Eastern Orthodoxy.

2300 BCE
The Rigveda begins to form in India – an early root of Hinduism

16th century CE
The Protestant Reformation leads to new branches of Christianity

19th century CE
The Baha'i Faith is founded in Persia, promoting unity and peace.

BCE stands for Before Common Era. It refers to the years before the year 1 in the Gregorian calendar, which is the calendar system most commonly used today. BCE is essentially the same as BC (Before Christ), but it is a non-religious or secular alternative.

CE stands for Common Era. It refers to the years from year 1 onwards. CE is equivalent to AD (Anno Domini, Latin for 'in the year of the Lord'), but again is a secular term.

What are the world's oldest religions?

When we talk about the oldest religions in the world, we are talking about belief systems that have shaped cultures, guided moral values, and influenced laws for thousands of years. These religions were born long before modern technology or global travel, and yet they are still followed by millions of people today. From ancient temples in India to mountain shrines in Japan, these religions continue to play an important role in people's lives across the world.

Let's take a look at some of the oldest religions that are still practised today.

Hinduism (circa 2500 BCE)

Country of origin: India

Number of followers today: Around 1.2 billion

Hinduism is often considered the world's oldest religion. While there is debate about exact dates, evidence of Hindu-like beliefs and rituals can be traced back as far as 7,000 BCE. It developed over thousands of years in what is now modern-day India and is closely tied to ancient texts known as the *Vedas*.

Hinduism is not based on the teachings of a single person. Instead, it includes a wide range of beliefs, gods, practices and traditions. Common themes include karma (the idea that actions have consequences), reincarnation (being reborn after death), and moksha (freedom from the cycle of rebirth). It has many gods and goddesses, with Brahma (the creator), Vishnu (the preserver) and Shiva (the destroyer) being some of the most important.

Judaism (circa 2000 BCE)

Country of origin: Middle East (Ancient Israel)

Number of followers today: Around 15 million

Judaism began over 4,000 years ago in the Middle East. It is based on the belief in one God and the teachings found in the *Torah*, the most sacred Jewish text. Abraham is considered the founder of Judaism, and the story of the Jewish people is closely tied to historical events like slavery in Egypt, the Exodus, and the building of the Temple in Jerusalem.

Jewish people follow religious laws and customs that have been passed down for centuries, including observing the Sabbath (a day of rest), celebrating festivals like Passover and Hanukkah, and following kosher dietary rules.

Zoroastrianism (circa 1500 BCE)

Country of origin: Persia (modern-day Iran)

Number of followers today: Around 100,000 to 200,000

Zoroastrianism was founded by the prophet Zoroaster (or Zarathustra) in ancient Persia. It was once one of the world's most powerful religions and was the official religion of the Persian Empire for hundreds of years.

Zoroastrians believe in one God, Ahura Mazda, and a constant battle between good and evil. Fire is a symbol of purity and is often used in Zoroastrian temples. Although the religion has declined over time, especially after the spread of Islam in Iran, it is still practised today, particularly in India (by the Parsi community) and in small communities in Iran.

Shinto (circa 700 BCE)

Country of origin: Japan

Number of followers today: Around 100 million

Shinto is the traditional religion of Japan and means 'the way of the gods.' It focuses on the worship of kami – spirits found in nature, objects and ancestors. Shinto has no single founder or central holy book. Instead, it is based on rituals and practices that connect people to nature, family and community.

Shrines are an important part of Shinto, where people go to pray, give thanks, or take part in ceremonies. Although many Japanese people also practise Buddhism, Shinto remains a key part of Japanese culture and identity.

Confucianism (circa 600 BCE)

Country of origin: China

Number of followers today: Around 6 million (with a broader influence on billions)

Confucianism is more of a philosophy than a religion, but it has deeply shaped Chinese culture and society for over 2,000 years. It was founded by Confucius, a Chinese teacher and philosopher who believed that people should live with honesty, respect, and loyalty to family and society.

Confucianism teaches the importance of education, kindness, and proper behaviour in relationships. Although not focused on gods or the afterlife, it includes ceremonies honouring ancestors and has been treated like a religion in many parts of East Asia.

Jainism (circa 600 BCE)

Country of origin: India

Number of followers today: Around 5 million

Jainism began in India around the same time as Buddhism. It teaches a path of non-violence, truth, and self-discipline. Jains believe that all living things – from people to insects – have souls and should not be harmed. Because of this, many Jains are strict vegetarians and some even wear masks to avoid accidentally breathing in tiny insects.

The religion was shaped by a teacher named Mahavira, who lived a simple, peaceful life and encouraged others to do the same. Although it is a smaller religion, Jainism has had a strong influence on Indian culture and ideas about compassion and peace.

Buddhism (circa 600 BCE)

Country of origin: India

Number of followers today: Around 500 million

Buddhism was founded by Siddhartha Gautama, known as the Buddha, who lived in India around the 6th century BCE. After years of searching for the meaning of life, he reached enlightenment under a tree and began to teach others how to overcome suffering.

Buddhism teaches the Four Noble Truths and the Eightfold Path as a way to achieve peace and freedom from suffering. It does not focus on worshipping gods but rather on personal spiritual growth. Today, Buddhism is practised in many countries, especially in Asia, and has many forms including Theravada, Mahayana and Zen.

Questions

1. Which religion is widely considered the world's oldest, and approximately when did it begin?
2. Which ancient religion began in Persia (modern-day Iran) and teaches about a constant battle between good and evil?
3. Name the Indian religion that teaches complete non-violence and encourages respect for all living beings, even the smallest insects.
4. In which religion would you learn about the Four Noble Truths and follow the Eightfold Path as a way to overcome suffering?
5. Which religion began in Japan and focuses on the worship of kami, or spirits found in nature and ancestors?
6. Who is considered the founding figure of Judaism?
7. How would you describe Confucianism, and what are its main values?
8. What ancient texts are closely linked to Hinduism, and what is one key belief in this religion?
9. What is the main teaching of Taoism about how people should live their lives?
10. Match each of these religions to its country of origin: Hinduism, Confucianism, Judaism, and Shinto.

Taoism (circa 500 BCE)

Country of origin: China

Number of followers today: Around 12 million

Taoism (also spelled Daoism) began in China and is based on the writings of Laozi, especially the *Tao Te Ching*. Tao means 'the Way,' and Taoists aim to live in harmony with the natural flow of the universe.

Taoism values simplicity, nature, and balance. It teaches that instead of fighting against problems, people should go with the flow, like water. Taoist temples, meditation, and traditional Chinese medicine are all part of this belief system, which still shapes Chinese culture today.

Why these religions still matter

Even after thousands of years, these religions continue to guide people's values, decisions and ways of life. Whether it's lighting candles at a Jewish festival, offering prayers at a Hindu temple, or practising mindfulness through Buddhism, these ancient traditions remain part of the modern world.

They also show how different cultures have asked the same big questions: Why are we here? What happens when we die? How should we treat others? Learning about the world's oldest religions helps us understand the beliefs of others – and think more deeply about our own.

Beyond beliefs: does religious faith lead to a happier, healthier life?

The stress-reducing, life-extending benefits of religion can offer useful strategies even for non-believers, say scientists.

By David Robson

In his *Pensées*, published posthumously in 1670, the French philosopher Blaise Pascal appeared to establish a foolproof argument for religious commitment, which he saw as a kind of bet. If the existence of God was even minutely possible, he claimed, then the potential gain was so huge – an 'eternity of life and happiness' – that taking the leap of faith was the mathematically rational choice.

Pascal's wager implicitly assumes that religion has no benefits in the real world, but some sacrifices. But what if there were evidence that faith could also contribute to better wellbeing? Scientific studies suggest this is the case. Joining a church, synagogue or temple even appears to extend your lifespan.

These findings might appear to be proof of divine intervention, but few of the scientists examining these effects are making claims for miracles. Instead, they are interested in understanding the ways that it improves people's capacity to deal with life's stresses. 'Religious and spiritual traditions give you access to different methods of coping that have distinctive benefits,' says Doug Oman, a professor in public health at the University of California Berkeley. 'From the psychological perspective, religions offer a package of different ingredients,' agrees Prof Patty Van Cappellen at Duke University in Durham, North Carolina.

Studying the life-extending benefits of religious practice can therefore offer useful strategies for anyone – of any faith or none – to live a healthier and happier life. You may find yourself shaking your head in scepticism, but the evidence base linking faith to better health has been decades in the making and now encompasses thousands of studies. Much of this research took the form of longitudinal research, which involves tracking the health of a population over years and even decades. They each found that measures of someone's religious commitment, such as how often they attended church, were consistently associated with a range of outcomes, including a lower risk of depression, anxiety and suicide and reduced cardiovascular disease and death from cancer.

Unlike some other areas of scientific research suffering from the infamous 'replication crisis', these studies have examined populations across the globe, with remarkably consistent results. And the effect sizes are large. Dr Laura Wallace at the University of Chicago Booth School of Business, for instance, recently examined obituaries of more than 1,000 people across the US and looked at whether the article recorded the person's religious affiliation – a sign that their faith had been a major element of their identity.

Publishing her results in 2018, she reported that those people marked out for their faith lived for 5.6 years more, on average, than those whose religion had not been recorded; in a second sample, looking specifically at a set of obituaries from Des Moines in Iowa, the difference was even greater – about 10 years in total. 'It's on par with the avoidance of major health risks – like smoking,' says Wallace. To give another comparison: reducing hypertension adds about five years to someone's life expectancy.

Health effects of this size demand explanation and scientists such as Wallace have been on the case. One obvious explanation for these findings is that people of faith live cleaner lives than the non-religious: studies show that churchgoers are indeed less likely to smoke, drink, take drugs or practise unsafe sex than people who do not attend a service regularly (though there are, of course, notable exceptions).

This healthier living may be the result of the religious teaching itself, which tends to encourage the principles of moderation and abstinence. But it could also be the fact that religious congregations are a self-selecting group. If you have sufficient willpower to get out of bed on a Sunday morning, for example, you may also have enough self-control to resist life's other temptations.

Importantly, however, the health benefits of religion remain even when the scientists have controlled for these differences in behaviour, meaning that other factors must also contribute. Social connection comes top of the list. Feelings of isolation and loneliness are a serious source of stress in themselves and exacerbate the other challenges we face in life. Even something as simple as getting to work becomes far more difficult if you cannot call on a friend to give you a lift when your car breaks down.

Chronic stress response can result in physiological changes such as heightened inflammation, which, over the years, can damage tissue and increase your risk of illness. As a result, the size of someone's social network and their subjective sense of connection with others can both predict their health and longevity, with one influential study by Prof Julianna Holt-Lunstad at Brigham Young University suggesting that the influence of loneliness is comparable to that of obesity or low physical exercise.

Religions, of course, tend to be built around a community of like-minded worshippers who meet regularly and have a shared set of beliefs. And many of the specific rituals will also contribute to a sense of communion with others. Christians, for example, are encouraged to pray on behalf of other people and this seems to bring its own health benefits, according to a brand new study by Prof Gail Ironson at the University of Miami.

Ironson has spent decades studying the ways that people with HIV cope with their infection and the influences of these psychological factors on the outcomes of disease. Examining data covering 17 years of 102 HIV patients' lives, she found that people who regularly prayed for others were twice as likely to survive to the end of the study, compared with those who more regularly prayed for themselves. Importantly, the link remained even after Ironson had accounted for factors such as adherence to medications or substance abuse or the patient's initial viral load.

Besides encouraging social connection, religion can help people to cultivate positive emotions that are good for our mental and physical wellbeing, such as gratitude and awe. Various studies show that regularly counting your blessings can help you to shift your focus away from the problems you are facing, preventing you from descending into the negative spirals of thinking that amplify stress. In the Christian church, you may be encouraged to thank God in your prayers, which encourages the cultivation of this protective emotion. 'It's a form of cognitive reappraisal,' says Van Cappellen. 'It's helping you to re-evaluate your situation in a more positive light.'

Awe, meanwhile, is the wonder we feel when we contemplate something much bigger and more important than ourselves. This can help people to cut through self-critical, ruminative thinking and to look beyond their daily concerns, so that they no longer make such a dent on your wellbeing.

Last, but not least, religious faiths can create a sense of purpose in someone's life – the feeling that there is a reason and meaning to their existence. People with a sense of purpose tend to have better mental wellbeing, compared with those who feel that their lives lack direction, and – once again – this seems to have knock-on effects for physical health, including reduced mortality. 'When people have a core set of values, it helps establish goals. And when those goals are established and pursued, that produces better psychological wellbeing,' says Prof Eric Kim at the University of British Columbia, who has researched the health benefits of purpose in life. Much like awe and gratitude, those positive feelings can then act as a buffer to stress.

These are average effects, which don't always take into account the huge variety of people's experiences. While some Christians might see God as a benevolent figure, others might have been taught that he is judgmental and punishing and those views can make a big difference in the effects on our health. In her studies of HIV patients, Ironson found that people who believed in a vengeful God showed a faster disease progression – as measured by their declining white blood cell count – compared with those who believed that he was a merciful figure.

Ultimately, most people's faith will arise from real convictions; it seems unlikely that many people would adopt a particular religious view solely for the health benefits. But even if you are agnostic, like me, or atheist, this research might inform your lifestyle.

You can start by considering contemplative techniques, which come in many more forms than the mindful breathing and body-scan techniques that have proved so popular. Scientists have become increasingly interested in 'loving-kindness meditation', for example, in which you spend a few moments thinking warm thoughts about friends, strangers, even enemies. The practice was inspired by the Buddhist principle of mettā, but it also resembles the Christian practice of intercessory prayer. When practised regularly, this increases people's feelings of social connection and empathy with the consequent benefits for their mental health. Importantly, it also changes people's real-life actions towards others, for instance encouraging more pro-social behaviour.

> **The power of religion is that it gives you this package of ingredients that are pre-made and organised for you**
>
> – Prof Patty Van Cappellen

To build more gratitude into your life, meanwhile, you might keep a diary listing the things that you have appreciated each day and you can make a deliberate habit of thanking the people who have helped you; both strategies have been shown to improve people's stress responses and to improve overall wellbeing. And to cultivate awe, you might go on a regular nature walk, visit a magnificent building within your city or watch a film that fills you with wonder.

If you have time and resources for greater commitments, you could also take up a voluntary activity for a cause that means a lot to you, a task that may help to boost your sense of purpose and which could also enhance your social life. Dr Wallace's work has shown that the sheer amount of volunteering someone performs could, independently, explain part of the longevity boost of religious people, but charitable actions do not need to be linked to a particular faith for you to gain those benefits. 'If people are able to plug into causes that really light up their intrinsic values, and then find a community that helps them reach their goals, that's another way in which the framework of religion can be taken into a non-religious context,' says Prof Kim.

The challenge is to ensure that you build all these behaviours into your routine, so that you perform them with the same regularity and devotion normally reserved for spiritual practices. 'The power of religion is that it gives you this package of ingredients that are pre-made and organised for you,' says Van Cappellen. 'And if you are not religious you have to create it on your own.' You don't need to make a leap of faith to see those benefits.

3 December 2022

Belief

Religious systems often include beliefs about the world (both seen and unseen), which describe (or dictate) how the world operates. Subscribing to a set of beliefs (orthodoxy) is not always essential for belonging to a religion.

By Luke Burns

Believing in the unseen

One of the most prominent and well-known aspects of religion in the Western world is faith. This term often comes with a variety of associated meanings and implications, but at its root we can say that faith involves belief in a set of doctrines or creeds which provide meaning and direction, often in the absence of empirical evidence.

Since the relationship between religious belief and scientific empiricism has often been contentious, it's worthwhile looking a little more closely at how people believe in things, and what this means.

There are different types of belief, and not all of them are considered religious; for example, very few of us have examined cells under microscopes, but we are all (I think!) happy to accept the idea that humans are composed of vast colonies of cellular creatures working in chemical harmony. Exceptionally few have been into space, but the image of the world as a floating globe orbiting a fiery nuclear reactor is almost universally taken as fact.

In fact, almost all of the scientific knowledge that is presented to school children, readers of popular science books, and the average person who takes an interest in such matters, is taken purely on faith. Most people simply don't have the means, skill, or inclination to personally verify all of the claims they would need to 'fact check' everything they are told. This faith is placed in the educational establishment, scientific community, and social authority – in other words, in people.

There is nothing inherently wrong with this approach to gaining knowledge about the world, and there are many checks and balances built into the scientific process to help reduce the ingress of error and personal bias, but it does present an interesting parallel to religious belief. Religious belief is often presented in such a way that it cannot be experimentally verified – even if we had all the resources of a modern university. A good example is the belief that Jesus was the son of God, and that he's capable of granting spiritual salvation. There is no DNA test that can prove this claim, and no scientific way to test that someone's soul has been saved (or indeed that one's soul exists at all). However, this is not entirely true.

Many religions encourage prospective adherents to test their claims through spiritual activities such as the reading of scripture, meditation, or other activities which encourage a religious mindset. For example, the Church of Jesus Christ of Latter-Day Saints (also known as the Mormons) sometimes refer to a passage in the *Book of Mormon* that instructs individuals to ask God whether the text is true to help resolve any doubts.

'And when ye shall receive these things, I would exhort you that ye would ask God, the Eternal Father, in the name of Christ, if these things are not true; and if ye shall ask with a sincere heart, with real intent, having faith in Christ, he will manifest the truth of it unto you, by the power of the Holy Ghost.' – The Book of Moroni 10.4, *Book of Mormon*

We find a similar claim in the *Qur'an*, which argues that its quality as scripture proves its authenticity, but challenges anyone to produce a work of comparable quality in order to refute it.

'Or do they say [about the Prophet], "He invented it?" Say, "Then bring forth a surah like it and call upon [for assistance] whomever you can besides Allah, if you should be truthful".' – *Qur'an* 10.38

In the *Qur'an*, each chapter is called a surah, so the verse here is arguing quite strongly that no one could create something equal to just a small portion of the *Qur'an*, even if they had help.

In the *Bhagavad Gita*, a Hindu text which takes the form of a conversation between the God Krishna and his devotee Arjuna, Krishna outright states that experience will resolve the doubts that come from reading different scriptures, with different ideas and values.

'When thy mind leaves behind its dark forest of delusion, thou shalt go beyond the scriptures of times past and still to come.

When thy mind, that may be wavering in the contradictions of many scriptures, shall rest unshaken in divine contemplation, then the goal of Yoga is thine.' – *Bhagavad Gita* 2.52-3 (trans. Mascaro)

And in the Sikh holy book, itself revered as a Guru, we find these comments originally composed by Guru Arjan:

'With one-pointed mind, meditate on the One Lord, and the doubts of your mind will be dispelled.' – *Sri Guru Granth Sahib* p. 47 (trans. Khalsa)

So, unlike scientific belief, which rests on evidence that can be tested publicly and repeatedly, religious belief tends to involve evidence that is personal, subjective, and unique to one moment in time – for example a response to a prayer or a moment of spiritual enlightenment.

This absence of scientific evidence does not necessary invalidate the truth claims made by religious traditions, but does change the nature of the relationship between the religious adherent and the truth, purpose, and beauty of their beliefs.

For example, some historians question whether Jesus (whether man or deity) actually existed, since the Gospels were written long after his death, and there are barely any independent references to him from the period in which he lived. Yet, despite this lack of strong material evidence, many millions of people across the world believe in the reality of Jesus, and his life as described in the *New Testament*; in fact, this belief has become so central to Christianity that it is difficult to define someone as Christian if they don't believe it, and it's part of one of the earliest formulations of the Christian religion: the Apostles' Creed:

'I believe in God, the Father almighty,

maker of heaven and earth;

And in Jesus Christ his only Son our Lord;

who was conceived by the Holy Ghost,

born of the Virgin Mary,

suffered under Pontius Pilate,

was crucified, dead, and buried.

He descended into hell.

The third day he rose again from the dead.

He ascended into heaven,

and sitteth on the right hand of God the Father almighty.

From thence he shall come to judge the quick and the dead.

I believe in the Holy Ghost,

the holy catholic Church,

the communion of saints,

the forgiveness of sins,

the resurrection of the body,

and the life everlasting. Amen.' – The Apostles' Creed

Some atheists and agnostics, who struggle with the the relationship between religious belief and empirical evidence, but who nonetheless were raised in a predominantly Christian culture and identify with some elements of the tradition, prefer to call themselves 'cultural Christians' – see for example Alana Massey's discussion on this and Trevin Wax's commentary for a Christian perspective.

There is a technical word for describing the way that some people insist on believing the 'right' things. Orthodoxy: strict adherence to a set of beliefs and principles.

Just like we found with 'belief', orthodoxy can also be used in non-religious contexts, wherever individuals are expected to follow a particular way of thinking or believing. For example, scientific orthodoxy is sometimes used to describe the way that certain ideas are so central to a scientific world view that they should not be questioned – like the spherical nature of the planet, or the absence of deities in the creation of the universe.

Due to the historical influence of Christianity in western nations, and the importance of orthodox belief structures to Christianity's success, there is a firm link between the idea of belief and the idea of religion in a western setting. Therefore, it's often a normal line of enquiry when learning about an unfamiliar religious tradition to ask 'what do they believe?'

However, belief was not always so central. In her TED talk, My Wish: The Charter for Compassion, author Karen Armstrong makes the point that prior to the 17th Century, the meaning of belief, and the significance it held in religious circles, was much different. It meant only to hold dear, or to prize, and the sense that people should hold a particular set of ideas about reality was not an enforced standard, as it later came to be.

It's not just pre-modern Christianity that has a more relaxed approach to belief; in many modern religious traditions it's not seen as important to subscribe to a specific set of ideas, but it often is important to engage in ritual practices or affirm identity with the community. Scholars have historically looked for ways to define religion according to 'belief' for the same reasons they have looked for books of religious law and ignored oral traditions, material culture, and lived experience – i.e., they represent a western understanding of Christian-centric religion as it was around the 19th and early 20th century when the science of religious studies was developing.

Though these belief-focused approaches are no longer common, they have nonetheless left a mark on the subject in the wider culture, and people may often think of a religion in terms such as Buddhists believe X rather than Buddhists do Y, or feel Z. It's not that belief isn't important, it's just that it's not the whole story.

1 January 2020

The above information is reprinted with kind permission from Understanding Religion.

www.understandingreligion.org.uk

How many religions are there?

When we think of religion, we might first picture the most well-known faiths like Christianity, Islam, Hinduism or Judaism. But religion is far more diverse than just a few global names. In fact, there are thousands of religions around the world – some with millions of followers, and others with only a handful of believers.

A religion is usually a set of beliefs about life, the universe, and a higher power or powers. It often involves practices such as prayer, rituals, celebrations, and a shared way of life. While some religions have been around for thousands of years, others are much newer. New spiritual movements and belief systems continue to emerge all the time.

Worldwide, scholars estimate there are more than 4,000 recognised religions. These include large, organised faiths as well as smaller, less formal belief systems. In the UK, the 2021 census asked people about their religion, and most respondents chose one of the major world religions – with Christianity still being the most common response, followed by Islam, Hinduism, Sikhism, Judaism and Buddhism.

But the census also allowed people to write in their own answers. Some people used this opportunity to express different kinds of belief – or even to have a bit of fun. One of the most surprising results came from the 2001 census, when over 390,000 people in England and Wales described their religion as 'Jedi'. This is a reference to the Jedi knights from the *Star Wars* films. It started as an internet campaign encouraging people to list 'Jedi' as a joke, but the number of people who did it was so large that it became the fourth most common response to the religion question in that year. Although it is not officially recognised as a religion by the government, some people have taken it more seriously and do consider Jediism to be a real spiritual path.

So, what makes something a religion? This is a difficult question to answer. Some people define religion as a belief in a God or gods, but not all religions are theistic (based on belief in a god). Buddhism, for example, does not focus on worshipping a God but rather on personal spiritual development. Others think religion is about a shared set of moral or philosophical ideas, or about belonging to a community with common values and traditions.

Because religion is so personal and varied, it is hard to give a single definition that covers everything. What is clear is that religion plays an important role in many people's lives, whether that means attending a place of worship, celebrating religious festivals, or simply following a set of beliefs that bring meaning and purpose.

In the end, the number of religions in the world is always changing, as people continue to explore big questions about life, death, and what it means to be human. Whether traditional or modern, serious or satirical, religion reflects the diversity of human thought and imagination.

The core teachings of the 5 major world religions

By CJ Faderogao

I recently visited a Buddhist temple. And while engrossing myself in the temple's beauty and sacred atmosphere, I was reminded of the diversity of faiths that we have on the world. We have faiths dating back thousands of years that we have cling into for comfort, hope, and personal peace. Both eastern and western culture had their roots in religions that shaped not only civilisation but also our early understanding of the human condition. For the longest time, these religions served as our moral and spiritual guides.

Given this, I find it inviting to revisit some of these faiths; explore and wonder about their messages, appreciate their ties with our culture, and ponder on their doctrines that have captured the heart and mind of man for centuries.

Here are the core teachings of the five major world religions:

Buddhism

Let's start with Buddhism. This religion originated from India, from the teachings of Siddhartha Gautama. Born a prince, he chose to live a spiritual life after witnessing the suffering of people outside the comforts of his palace. He spent his life grappling with the question of why man must suffer, and hoped to find a way out of it.

After years of solitude and inquiry, he determined that both neglecting one's needs (ascetism) and, on the other hand, indulging in pleasure (hedonism) can't lead to spiritual emancipation. Rather, he found out that the best path to take is one of moderation, one the Buddhists call the middle way. In this frame of mind is how Siddhartha eventually became enlightened, he has attained what Buddhists call Nirvana (a state of perfect happiness and peace) while sitting in the now famous Bodhi Tree.

Siddhartha realised the core teachings of Buddhism called The four noble truths and devised the Eight-fold path, a set of actions that leads one to Enlightenment.

The Four Noble Truths are:

1. Suffering is inevitable in life.
2. The root of our suffering is our desires and attachment to impermanent things.
3. Our suffering can be ended by the cessation of these attachments.
4. In order to bring this about, we must follow the Eight-fold path.

The Eight-Fold path includes:

1. Having a right view. (Commitment to truth)
2. Having the right intentions. (Commitment to spiritual life)
3. Having right speech. (Speak no evil)
4. Having right actions. (Being ethical and non-indulgent)
5. Having a right livelihood. (Having a respectful job; living in moderation)
6. Having right effort. (Acting with a clear conscience)
7. Having right mindfulness. (Taking responsibility for one's thoughts)
8. Having right concentration. (A life spent in meditation)

Islam

Islam, translated in English as 'submission,' was founded by the Prophet Muhammad. It has Arabic roots, and its centre of worship is in Mecca, Saudi Arabia. For most of his life, Muhammad was a merchant but he was also interested in the mysteries of faith. At age 40, while meditating in a cave, he saw visions given by the angel Gabriel (the same Gabriel from the Christian faith). These revelations would be compiled and would become what we know of as the *Quran*.

Islam is a monotheistic faith. Muslims call god Allah, translated in English as 'the God.' They consider prophets like Muhammad as messengers of God rather than people to be worshipped. Their priests, called Imam, acts in this way by serving as leaders in interpreting the *Quran*.

The core beliefs of Islam are:

1. Allah is the one true God.
2. Prophets are messengers of God, and Muhammad is the best and the last one. (Unbeknownst to many, Islam acknowledges Jesus, Moses, David and, other figures of the Christian faith as real prophets).
3. Angels are real. Like Prophets, they act as messengers of God.
4. Angels and prophets are mediums for revelations. Through them, the word and will of Allah are brought about. These revelations can be found in the *Quran*, which contains the literal words of Allah.
5. There will be a day of judgment. At the end times, Allah will punish the wicked and reward the virtuous.

In living, they have the five core pillars of Islam as their guide:

1. Shahada: The profession of faith. (Believing that there is only one God: Allah, and Muhammad is his last prophet).
2. Salah: Prayer. (Praying five times a day facing Mecca).
3. Zakat: Charity. (Helping people in need. Muslims are decreed to share 2.5% of their wealth to the poor).
4. Sawm: Fasting. (Done during Ramadan, a month, which Muslims believed Muhammad got his revelations).
5. Hajj: Pilgrimage to Mecca. (If able, a Muslim must visit Mecca, the centre of their faith, once in their lifetime).

Hinduism

Though still debated, Hinduism is considered the oldest of the 5 major world religions. Today, it remains to be a faith diverse in itself, symbolised by multiple gods, and multiple ways of worshipping them. Hinduism also originated in India but predates Buddhism for thousands of years.

Hindus, like Christianity, have a trinity that they adhere to. Their main Gods are Brahma (the creator), Vishnu (the preserver), and Shiva (the destroyer). Hindus believe that the universe is made of a single thing called Brahman – the true and eternal essence of everything. One of the main goals of the faith is to bring people back into this essence, merging into its totality and escaping the cycle of Samsara or rebirth.

A well-known concept relating to this cycle is karma. Hinduism preserves the idea that each of us are souls being reincarnated since the beginning of time. Having good karma (good action) ensures one's reincarnation will be a pleasant one. Bad karma, on the other hand, can cause one to be reincarnated in a lowly form.

Hinduism's holy texts are called the *Vedas*. They are believed to be written by ancient prophets through revelations. The *Vedas* are composed of four main books but over time become accompanied by now more famous texts such as the *Upanishads*, the *Bhagavad Gita*, and the epics *Ramayana* and *Mahabharata*.

The other principles of Hinduism include:

1. Dharma: Hindus believed that each life has their own Dharma, a duty which should be fulfilled as decreed by Brahman. A singer's dharma is to sing, a swimmer to swim, and a teacher, to teach.
2. Atman: Hindus call people's soul Atman. It is immortal and is the one subjected to karma and rebirth.
3. Caste: A social order decreed by the *Vedas* stating the way society must be structured. The are five main castes: Brahmins (priests), Kshatriya (warriors), Vaishya (merchants), and Sudras (peasants).
4. Moksha: Hindus' ideal of spiritual release. An individual who has attained moksha is now at one with Brahman.

In order to attain spiritual liberation, Hindus practice:

- Fulfilling their dharma.
- Gaining Artha. (Economic and Material stability).
- Kama. (Desire for love and emotional wellbeing).
- Moksha. (The culmination of the other virtues and the goal of the religion itself).

Christianity

Christians comprise 33.11% of the present world population. It is the most widespread and accepted religion in many parts of the world. The Christian faith is founded upon the teaching of Jesus Christ, a spiritual teacher from Nazareth, Israel. Christians consider Jesus as the Messiah – their saviour from sins. During his time, Jesus performed miracles and preached spiritual lessons to people around Israel. The greatest miracle of them all being his supposed resurrection after his death. His resurrection is the basis for another core principle called the good news, declaring all people to rejoice because Jesus proved that there's life beyond death.

Jesus's works was chronicled in four books called the *Gospels*, which comprises the majority of the whole Christian texts called *The New Testament*. Christian belief is structured into classifying God as a Trinity. They maintain that God has three personas: the Father, the Son, and the Holy Spirit.

Other pillars of the Christian faith includes:

- The Pope: The present leader of the Church, ruling in succession starting from Peter, one of Jesus' Twelve Disciples.
- The Virgin Mary: Mother of Jesus Christ, whom in turn became known as the mother of the church.
- Christmas Day: Celebrated on 25th December each year. A day spent in honour of Jesus Christ's birth.
- Holy Week: A week spent remembering the suffering and resurrection of Jesus Christ.

To live by their faith, Christians practice the seven Sacraments:

1. Baptism: A rite of washing away sins and welcoming a person to the Christian faith.
2. Eucharist: Also called communion. A ceremony during mass where Christians remember Christ's sacrifice by eating a bread (symbolising Jesus's body) and drinking wine (symbolising Jesus's blood).
3. Confirmation: An affirmation of one's faith, often performed when one is matured enough to understand and commit to the Christian way of life.
4. Confession: Absolving of one's sins by confessing to a priest and asking for God's forgiveness.
5. Anointing of the sick: A blessing done to those who are in old age or to those who are nearing death because of sickness.
6. Marriage: The blessed union of a man and a woman becoming husband and wife.
7. The Holy Order: The profession of becoming a priest.

Judaism

Judaism is a monotheistic religion that also originated in the Middle East. It is the religion of the Jewish people of present day Israel. According to Jewish lore, the faith started when a man named Abraham entered a covenant with a God called Yahweh, promising Abraham of a pleasant future along with his descendants. Abraham was then commanded to take his family into the promised land (Israel) to live there and prosper.

The holy scriptures of Judaism are called the *Tanakh* and it is comprised of 3 main texts: the *Ketuvim*, *Nevi'im*, and the most widely known, the *Torah*. The *Torah* is composed of five books (*Genesis, Exodus, Leviticus, Numbers*, and *Deuteronomy*) chronicling the history, journey, and relationship of the Jews with Yahweh. Other prominent figures in Jewish faith includes Moses, King David, King Solomon, and Jacob.

Jews consider God as a single entity, all powerful, all knowing, and ever present. A benevolent law giver akin to a father, forever caring for the welfare of his people. Jewish practices are often convergent with their history. They perform rituals and acts in remembrance of their ancestors. Some notable examples are the Feast of Passover (commemorating Jews' freedom from Egyptian enslavement), the Hanukkah (a festival for the recovery of Jerusalem, Jews' holy city) and Sabbath (resting on the 7th day of the week just like Yahweh in the story of creation).

Other components of Jewish faith include:

- Rabbis: Their master of ceremonies and spiritual leaders. They help interpret and preach the message of the *Tanakh*.
- Synagogue: Jews' place of worship.
- Menorah: A seven branched candle used during rituals and festivities.
- The Star of David: A hexagram symbol for Jewish identity and faith.

These religions continue to be subjects of curiosity, study, and worship today. The literatures, practices and customs that have sprung up from them remains embedded and ingrained in mankind's collective psyche. They are undeniable parts of our history, culture, and identity. Most importantly, they are reminders for us to seek our spiritual-wellbeing, no matter what practice or faith we are drawn to to find it.

18 May 2023

Questions

1. What is the main belief about God in Christianity, and how is Jesus viewed?
2. How does Islam describe the relationship between humans and Allah?
3. What are the Four Noble Truths in Buddhism?
4. In Hinduism, what role does karma play in a person's life?
5. What does Judaism teach about the importance of laws and commandments?

Compare and contrast

Compare and contrast two religions mentioned in the article. Create a table showing at least three similarities and three differences in their teachings.

Make a glossary

Make a glossary of at least ten key terms found in the article (e.g. *Torah*, karma, nirvana), with definitions in your own words.

Design a poster

Choose one of the religions in this article and create a poster summarising the core belief

Discuss

In small groups, discuss how understanding different religions might help reduce prejudice and promote respect in a school or community setting.

The world religions paradigm

When the category of religion is used to describe 'world religions', it is often in a way that turns multiple diverse traditions, philosophies, and practices into one single entity for the sake of simplicity.

By Luke Burns

When the category of religion is used to describe 'world religions', it is often in a way that turns multiple diverse traditions, philosophies, and practices into one single entity for the sake of simplicity.

A good example of this is Hinduism, which is a label coined by the British to describe the religion of the Indian people.

The hidden diversity of Hinduism

Hinduism did not exist in the language of the Indian peoples (in fact there are many languages in use on the Indian subcontinent); it was a label applied by British observers.

There are many different religious traditions in India that are viewed as subdivisions within Hinduism, but this shared definition does not mean that all Hindus believe the same things or practice in the same way.

Of course, Hinduism (as a category) has been in use for so long now that many Hindus are perfectly happy using it to describe their religious affiliation, but not all feel the same way, and it is a good example of the sort of effect that using alien terminology can have when describing a culture other than one's own. The scope for misunderstanding is wide, and it is easy to make mistakes that have repercussions for hundreds of years.

Recognising difference

The issue remains that it is far too easy to talk about 'religion X' as though it is one single group of people, who all believe the same things and act the same way – but this is clearly not true.

In Europe and North America, most people have grown up with exposure to the differences between Christian denominations (certainly the differences between Catholic and Protestant forms of worship). This nuanced understanding is less widespread when it comes to traditions that are not native to one's culture, or with which one has less experience.

In other words, the less you know about a religious tradition, the easier it is to make generalisations and assumptions. If we take these generalisations to be fact, then we're in dangerous territory.

Who makes the cut?

In addition to smoothing over subtle differences within a religious tradition, the designation of something as a 'World Religion' is also often used to restrict what counts as a religion. Many people have inherited a list of the 'big players' like Christianity, Islam, Buddhism, Judaism, and Hinduism.

However, this approach ignores a vast range of religious systems, especially indigenous traditions.

It ignores, and encourages others to ignore, many vibrant and diverse expressions of human religiosity.

Religion or religions?

As a remedy for this singular approach to constructing religions, some scholars have argued that it is more appropriate to talk about religion in the plural: Hinduisms, Buddhisms, Christianities.

'In 1963 Wilfred Cantwell Smith wrote, "I seriously suggest that terms such as Christianity, Buddhism, and the like must be dropped, as clearly untenable once challenged". He argued that the world had Buddhists but not Buddhism, Christians but not Christianity, and so forth. Smith suggested the word "religion" be dropped as well, claiming that monolithic terms such as "religion," "Christianity," "Hinduism" obscure the dynamic and personal quality of religious traditions.' – Urubshurow, 2008, p. xix

Writing in *Buddhisms: An Introduction*, John Strong makes a similar argument, and suggests the use of the split singular/plural formation Buddhism/s. He points out that there are many points at which Buddhist traditions converge, yet these are also sites of contested meaning and disagreement.

'It is sometimes said that one of the things that holds Buddhism/s together is the fact that, either explicitly or implicitly, Buddhists all turn to the "three refuges" or "triple gem" of the tradition: the Buddha, his Teaching (called the dharma), and his community (called the sangha). At the same time, however, it must be recognised that the Buddha, dharma, and sangha can mean different things to different Buddhists, so that while the three refuges may unite Buddhists everywhere, they also divide them.' – Strong, 2015, p. 18

This convention reminds us that what we are looking at is a diverse group of traditions and practices that do not necessarily agree with each other – one only has to look at the differences between denominations of Christianity to understand that a single label is not sufficient.

Many Eucharists

As an example, we could look at the differences between a Protestant and Eastern Orthodox ceremony known as the Eucharist.

To begin with, let's look at the original passage in the *Book of Luke*, one of the core Christian texts that describe the life of Jesus:

'After taking the cup, he gave thanks and said, "Take this and divide it among you. For I tell you I will not drink again from the fruit of the vine until the kingdom of God comes." And he took bread, gave thanks and broke it, and gave it to them, saying, "This is my body given for you; **do this in remembrance of me**." In the same way, after the supper he took the cup, saying, "This cup is the new covenant in my blood, which is poured out for you."' – *Luke* 22:17-20

I've added the emphasis to the line where Jesus specifically instructs his followers to perform the act of eating and drinking in remembrance.

Now let's look at a description of the modern sacrament as celebrated by the Orthodox Church in America:

The first action of the liturgy is the gathering in common. The baptised and confirmed gather in one place. After the common prayer of the Church called the Great Litany in which petitions are made for all of the essential elements of life, biblical *psalms* are sung and the Word of God is presented to the faithful. Here the emphasis is on the epistle, the gospel and the sermon.

Then follows the offering of the bread and the wine as the offering of ourselves and our world to God in Christ. We ask God to accept us and our gifts (the bread and wine) as we love one another and confess the Orthodox faith, the Nicene Creed which we, or our sponsors for us, proclaimed at our baptism.

We then offer up ourselves and our gifts to God in Christ in remembrance of all that He has done for us: the cross, the tomb, the resurrection of the third day, the Ascension into heaven, the sitting on the right hand of God the father, and the second and glorious coming again.

We then call the Holy Spirit "to come upon us and upon our gifts" and to make them the Body and Blood of Christ and to give us the experience of the Kingdom of Heaven. Thus we receive back our gifts of bread and wine as the gift of Holy Communion with God the Father through Christ and the Spirit.

Finally we depart in peace to bear witness in the world to the Kingdom of God which has been given to us, calling all men into this unity with God and each other in Him.

The Orthodox celebrate this Mystery of the Kingdom of God, the Divine Liturgy on each Lord's Day as well as on feasts and special occasions. It is the living experience of what all Christianity, and indeed all of life, is really about. [1]

Finally, let's look at how the Eucharist is celebrated by a Protestant church, in this case Barnstaple Baptist Church, in Devon, UK:

'Our celebration is simple and straightforward. We take it at Sunday services twice a month. We take Communion because Jesus indicated that we should do it in order to remember Him. (see: 1 *Corinthians* 11:23-36).

The Communion involves each Believer taking and eating a small piece of bread from a shared loaf. The bread symbolises and represents the body of the Lord Jesus Christ which He gave in the sacrifice of crucifixion for us.

The Communion also involves each Believer taking and drinking from a glass of wine or juice. The wine symbolises and represents the blood of the Lord Jesus Christ which He shed in the sacrifice of crucifixion for us.

By submitting to crucifixion Jesus procured for us the forgiveness and the cleansing of our sins and the salvation which gives us new life in His Holy Spirit.

In taking the Communion together we keep ourselves ever mindful of what Jesus has done for us. Unlike some churches, we do not believe that prayers over the bread and the wine change (or transubstantiate) them into the actual flesh and the actual blood of Jesus. We believe they are to be understood as symbols.' [2]

Although there are some key features in common with both services (eating the bread, drinking the wine), there are some interesting differences in how these acts are presented. For the Orthodox Church, the eating and drinking happen almost immediately, followed by a series of ritual actions designed to indicate surrender to God, remembrance of Jesus, and petition to receive 'the gift of Holy Communion'. There is a sense that something mysterious and powerful is taking place, and that the bread and wine act as doorways into a deeper and more spiritual relationship with God.

In contrast, the Baptist Church uses the scriptural passage to provide the context and rationale behind the ceremony, and the act is rooted in remembrance, there is no sense that the bread and wine take on any spiritual power in and of themselves – the ritual is for the purpose of remembering the life of Jesus, in the way that is instructed in the Gospel.

This is just one example of the internal diversity within religions. When we talk about 'Christianity', what we are really doing is taking the most obvious features from a number of different traditions and individuals, and creating a merged version that might be applicable to every Christian, but this approach not only misses out on crucial detail, it is so frequently wrong or misleading that it does very little to advance our understanding.

More important than understanding what each 'religion' teaches, or what a 'typical religious adherent' believes or does, is to approach each individual as a fresh and unique example of lived religion – to expect and look for a vast universe of religions, grounded in human experience and complexity.

The urge to generalise can definitely be of service, and there is often as much that unites different traditions as divides them, but we must be careful in how much we allow ourselves to blend out the differences for the sake of making blanket statements about entire religious groups.

30 October 2020

1. https://oca.org/questions/divineliturgy/the-divine-liturgy
2. https://www.barnstaplebaptist.org.uk/communion.htm

One world, many beginnings: creation myths and their meanings

From the beginning of time, people have asked big questions: Where did we come from? How did the world begin? What is our purpose? These are deep and meaningful questions, and across different cultures and times, religions have tried to answer them. Many of the world's major religions include a creation story – a way of explaining how everything began.

Although these stories differ in detail, they often share similar ideas. They explore the relationship between humans and the universe, the role of a divine creator or force, and how life came to be. Let's take a look at some of the key creation stories from the major world religions, and then explore what they have in common.

Christianity

In Christianity, the creation story is found at the beginning of the *Bible*, in the book of *Genesis*. Christians believe that God created the world in six days and rested on the seventh. The story goes like this:

On the first day, God created light and separated it from darkness.

On the second day, He created the sky.

On the third day, He formed land, seas, and plants.

On the fourth day, He made the sun, moon, and stars.

On the fifth day, He created sea creatures and birds.

On the sixth day, He made land animals and humans – Adam and Eve.

On the seventh day, God rested, and this is why Christians often rest or go to church on Sundays.

This story shows God as powerful, purposeful, and creative. Humans are made in God's image, which gives them a special place in creation. Christians believe that everything God made was 'good'.

Judaism

Judaism shares much of the same creation story as Christianity, as it also comes from the book of *Genesis*. This is because the Hebrew *Bible*, or *Tanakh*, includes *Genesis* as one of its books. In fact, Christianity grew out of Judaism, so the similarities make sense.

Like Christians, Jewish people believe that God created the world in six days and rested on the seventh. This idea is very important in Judaism, and the weekly day of rest, called Shabbat, begins on Friday evening and ends on Saturday evening. It reflects the belief that God's rest after creation is something to be honoured.

There are also Jewish interpretations that look more deeply into the meanings of the creation story. Some Jewish thinkers understand the story more symbolically than literally, seeing it as a poetic way of explaining truths about God and the world.

Islam

Islam also shares a similar creation story, although it comes from a different holy book – the *Qur'an*. In the *Qur'an*, God (called Allah in Arabic) is described as the one who created the heavens and the earth. The *Qur'an* does not lay out the creation in the same day-by-day structure as the *Bible*, but it does speak of Allah creating the world in six 'periods' or 'days'.

Muslims believe that Allah created everything with great care and wisdom. Like Christianity and Judaism, Islam teaches that humans are a special part of creation. The first human, Adam, is seen as a prophet and the first person to worship Allah.

The *Qur'an* also says that everything in creation is a sign of Allah's greatness. Nature, the stars, animals, and even our own bodies are seen as proof of a divine creator.

Hinduism

Hinduism is different from the three Abrahamic religions (Judaism, Christianity, and Islam) in many ways, including its creation stories. In Hinduism, there is not just one version of how the world began – there are many. Hindu texts such as the *Rig Veda*, one of the oldest sacred writings, include poetic and sometimes mysterious descriptions of the universe coming into being.

One story tells of a cosmic being called Purusha, whose body was sacrificed to create the world. From his mouth came the Brahmins (priests), from his arms the warriors, from his thighs the merchants, and from his feet the workers. This story is often used to explain the different groups or castes in Indian society.

Another story speaks of Brahma, the creator god, who creates the universe, while Vishnu preserves it and Shiva destroys it when the time comes. These three gods represent a cycle of creation, preservation, and destruction – which reflects the Hindu idea that the universe is constantly being born, dying, and being reborn.

Buddhism

Buddhism does not focus heavily on creation stories in the same way other religions do. This is because the teachings of the Buddha focus more on how to end suffering than how the world began. However, in some Buddhist texts, there are stories about the universe going through endless cycles of creation and destruction – a bit like in Hinduism.

In Buddhist cosmology, the universe has no clear beginning or end. Instead, it goes through cycles of expansion and contraction. Beings are born, die, and are reborn in different realms depending on their actions, or karma.

Because Buddhism is more about spiritual development and less about worshipping a creator god, creation stories are not central. Still, they reflect the Buddhist idea that everything changes and that nothing lasts forever.

Sikhism

Sikhism is a relatively young religion, founded in the 15th century in India. It teaches that there is one God who created the universe. The Sikh holy book, the *Guru Granth Sahib*, speaks of God as timeless and formless, and of creation as an expression of God's will.

Sikhism teaches that the universe came into being when God said, 'Let there be creation.' From that moment, everything appeared – the planets, stars, water, life, and humans. Sikhs do not believe that God then stepped back, but that God is still present in everything and everyone.

Like in other religions, creation is seen as a sign of God's greatness and creativity. Sikhs are encouraged to see the divine in the world around them.

What the stories have in common

Despite all the differences in detail, there are several striking similarities in the creation stories of major religions. Here are a few:

1. A beginning

All creation stories try to answer the question: how did everything begin? Whether it was in six days, through cycles of birth and rebirth, or through divine speech, they all point to a time when the world was not yet formed, and something brought it into being.

2. A creator or creative force

In almost every tradition, there is a creative force behind the universe. It may be a single God, many gods, or a mysterious energy. This shows a shared belief that the world did not simply appear by chance – it was made, shaped, or designed.

3. The special role of humans

Most creation stories include a moment when humans are made. In some stories, like those from Christianity, Judaism, and Islam, humans are made in God's image or are given a special purpose. In Hinduism and Buddhism, humans have a chance to grow spiritually. In indigenous traditions, humans are often seen as caretakers of the land.

4. A sense of order

Creation stories often describe the universe moving from chaos to order. Light is separated from darkness, land from water, good from bad. This reflects the human need to understand the world as a place that makes sense – a place where things are in the right place.

5. Moral or spiritual meaning

Finally, creation stories are not just about how the world began – they also carry messages. They teach people about their place in the universe, their relationship with others, and how they should live. For example, if the world is a gift from God, people might feel they should look after it. If life is full of cycles, they might try to act wisely to improve their future.

Why creation stories matter

Creation stories are a central part of most religions. They offer more than just an explanation of how the world began – they help people understand their place in the universe, their relationship with others, and how they should live. These stories have been told and retold across generations, often through sacred texts, storytelling traditions, and rituals. Their continued presence shows just how important they are to the human experience.

At their heart, creation stories try to answer some of life's biggest questions: Where did we come from? Why are we here? What is our purpose? In times before science offered explanations of the natural world, people used these stories to make sense of what they saw around them – the sky, the sea, the seasons, life and death. Even today, for many religious believers, these stories remain powerful and meaningful.

Creation stories also shape values. They often include moral or spiritual lessons about how to live. In some traditions, humans are created in the image of God, which suggests that every person has value, dignity, and purpose. In others, humans are placed on Earth to care for the natural world, encouraging respect for animals, plants, and the environment. In this way, creation stories influence not only personal beliefs but also behaviour and ethical choices.

They are also important for building a sense of identity and community. A creation story may tell a group of people where they came from, what they were created to do, or how they are connected to each other and to the land. This can create a shared sense of belonging and a deeper understanding of cultural or religious heritage.

Learning about different creation stories can help people understand each other better. While the details of these stories vary, many contain similar ideas – a divine force, a special role for humans, a sense of order from chaos. These shared themes show that people across the world and throughout history have asked similar questions and searched for meaning in similar ways.

Finally, creation stories remind us of the power of storytelling. Through vivid language, symbols, and imagination, they express deep truths about life, meaning, and hope. They remain relevant because they speak to something timeless – the human desire to understand and to belong.

Celebrations and festivals

Festivals and celebrations are important in every culture and religion around the world. They bring people together to share joy, express beliefs, honour traditions, and make lasting memories. For many young people, festivals are also a chance to learn more about their identity or to explore different ways of life. Whether religious or cultural, big or small, festivals help communities celebrate what matters to them most.

In this article, we will explore some of the main religious festivals from different faiths, as well as a few exciting cultural celebrations like Melas and Chinese New Year.

Mela

A Mela is a festival or fair that celebrates South Asian culture and community. The word Mela means 'gathering' or 'fair' in Sanskrit. In the UK, Melas are colourful events that often include music, food stalls, traditional dancing, fashion, and games. While some have religious roots, most are now cultural and open to people of all backgrounds. They are a great way to enjoy and learn about South Asian traditions.

Chinese New Year

Chinese New Year, also called the Spring Festival, marks the beginning of the lunar new year. It usually falls between January and February and is the biggest celebration in Chinese culture. Each year is linked to one of 12 zodiac animals.

Celebrations include red decorations, lanterns, firecrackers, family feasts, and giving red envelopes with money for good luck. In cities across the UK, dragon and lion dances often take place in parades. The festival ends with the Lantern Festival, where glowing lanterns light up the sky to bring hope for the year ahead.

Christian festivals

Christianity includes many important celebrations, with Christmas and Easter being the most widely observed.

Christmas on 25 December celebrates the birth of Jesus Christ. It is a time for church services, carols, family meals, and giving gifts. In the lead-up to Christmas, many Christians observe Advent, a four-week period of preparation. Advent calendars or candles are often used to count down the days.

Easter celebrates the resurrection of Jesus. The build-up to Easter is called Lent, which lasts for 40 days (excluding Sundays). Lent begins on Ash Wednesday, a day when Christians may attend a church service and receive a cross of ash on their forehead as a sign of reflection. Some people give something up during Lent to focus on what matters most.

The day before Lent begins is Shrove Tuesday, also known as Pancake Day, where people traditionally use up rich foods like eggs and sugar. Holy Week, which includes Good Friday and Easter Sunday, marks the final days of Jesus' life, his death, and his resurrection.

Orthodox Christian festivals

Orthodox Christians often follow a different calendar from Western Christians, so their key celebrations like Christmas and Easter fall on different dates.

Orthodox Christmas is usually celebrated on 7 January and Orthodox Easter on a different Sunday in spring, depending on the lunar calendar. Orthodox Easter is known for its long, beautiful church services, processions, and rituals. In many cultures, red-dyed eggs are cracked together as a symbol of life and victory over death.

Muslim festivals

Islam has two major religious celebrations: Eid al-Fitr and Eid al-Adha.

Eid al-Fitr is the festival that marks the end of Ramadan, a holy month when Muslims fast from dawn to sunset. It begins with a special prayer, followed by meals with family and friends, new clothes, and giving to charity.

Eid al-Adha, the Festival of Sacrifice, honours the prophet Ibrahim's willingness to sacrifice his son for God. It is marked by prayers and sharing meat with family, friends, and those in need.

Another important day is the Islamic New Year, or Hijri New Year, which marks the beginning of the Islamic calendar. It commemorates the migration (Hijra) of the Prophet Muhammad from Makkah to Madinah. The Islamic New Year is often observed with quiet reflection, prayer, and remembrance, rather than big celebrations.

Jewish festivals

Judaism includes several major festivals, many of which are based on historical events and religious teachings.

Hanukkah, the Festival of Lights, lasts for eight days. It remembers a time when a small amount of oil miraculously burned for eight nights in a rededicated temple. Families light candles on a menorah, one each night, and celebrate with food, games like dreidel, and gifts.

Passover (Pesach) remembers the Israelites' escape from slavery in Egypt. Jewish families hold a Seder meal where they read from the Haggadah, a special book that tells the story of the Exodus. Matzah, a type of flatbread, is eaten to remember how the Israelites left in such a hurry that their bread didn't have time to rise.

Rosh Hashanah, the Jewish New Year, marks the beginning of ten days of reflection, ending with Yom Kippur, the Day of Atonement. During this time, Jewish people reflect on the past year, say sorry for wrongdoings, and try to make a fresh start. Rosh Hashanah is celebrated with special prayers, apples dipped in honey, and the blowing of a ram's horn (shofar).

Sukkot is a harvest festival where families build and eat meals in temporary shelters (sukkahs) to remember their ancestors' journey through the desert.

Hindu festivals

Diwali, the Festival of Lights, celebrates the victory of good over evil and light over darkness. People decorate their homes with lamps, wear new clothes, visit temples, and enjoy sweets and fireworks.

Holi, the Festival of Colours, marks the arrival of spring. People throw coloured powders and water at each other in the streets, celebrating joy, playfulness, and togetherness. It is a time of fun, but also of forgiveness and new beginnings.

Sikh festivals

One of the most important Sikh festivals is Vaisakhi, which celebrates the formation of the Khalsa – the community of committed Sikhs – in 1699. It also marks the Punjabi New Year and the harvest season. In the UK, Vaisakhi processions (Nagar Kirtans) are lively events filled with singing, prayers, and free food.

Guru Nanak Gurpurab celebrates the birth of Guru Nanak, the founder of Sikhism. Sikhs mark the occasion with hymns, readings from the *Guru Granth Sahib*, and acts of kindness and service.

Buddhist festivals

Vesak, or Buddha Day, is the most important Buddhist festival. It celebrates the birth, enlightenment, and death of Gautama Buddha. Buddhists may visit temples, light candles, meditate, and practise generosity.

In some traditions, people release lanterns, birds, or fish to symbolise letting go of the past and wishing peace for all beings. Vesak is a calm and thoughtful celebration focused on compassion and mindfulness.

Why festivals matter

Festivals help us connect – with our faith, our family, and our communities. They remind us of stories, values, and traditions that matter deeply to many people. Whether it is lighting candles, fasting, feasting, dancing, or reflecting quietly, each celebration offers something special.

By learning about different festivals, we not only understand others better, but also learn more about the world we all share.

Compare

Choose two festivals from different religions and compare them.

Write a short paragraph (about 150–200 words) explaining:

- What each festival celebrates
- How each one is celebrated
- What values or beliefs they share

Design a celebration poster

Create a colourful, informative poster for a festival of your choice.

You may draw or use digital tools to make your poster visually appealing.

Guided by the moon: how faith follows the lunar cycle

When you look up at the night sky, you might see a full, glowing moon or just a thin silver crescent. It is beautiful, of course, but it is also deeply meaningful. For thousands of years, people have followed the movements of the moon to guide their lives. In many religions, the moon is more than a light in the sky – it is a way of marking sacred time.

Psalm 104 verse 19 says, 'He made the moon to mark the seasons.' This idea – that the moon has a purpose – can be found in several world religions. The moon helps people know when to fast, when to feast, when to reflect, and when to celebrate. In this article, we will explore how the moon helps shape some of the most important religious festivals celebrated in the UK today: Ramadan, Passover and Easter.

Why the moon matters in religion

The moon has long been used as a natural calendar. It takes around 29.5 days for the moon to complete its cycle – from new moon, to full moon, and back again. These regular phases make it easy to track time, especially before the invention of clocks and calendars. Some early civilisations even carved moon-shaped symbols into stones to help them remember the passage of months.

Many religions developed in societies that closely watched nature. The sun, stars and especially the moon were seen as signs from a higher power. The moon's cycle was linked to planting, harvesting, travelling and worship. Over time, many religious calendars were based on these lunar patterns.

The Islamic calendar is fully lunar – each month begins with the new moon. The Jewish calendar is lunisolar – meaning it follows the moon for months, but adjusts for the solar year to keep festivals in the same season. The Christian calendar is mostly solar, but still uses the moon to work out when Easter falls.

Religions also use the moon symbolically. The moon's steady cycle has become a reminder of change, reflection and renewal. As the moon disappears and returns again, it reflects the idea of spiritual growth and transformation. Watching the moon connects many people with a sense of peace, wonder, and belonging to something larger than themselves.

Ramadan and the Islamic calendar

In Islam, the calendar is completely based on the moon. Each new month begins when the new moon is sighted. This means the Islamic year is slightly shorter than the Gregorian calendar, so Islamic festivals move back by about 10 to 11 days each year.

Ramadan is the ninth month of the Islamic year and one of the most sacred times for Muslims. It begins when the new moon is seen and is confirmed by trusted religious authorities. During Ramadan, Muslims fast from dawn to sunset. That means no food or drink during the day. But it is about more than just fasting – it is a time of spiritual reflection, generosity, prayer and community.

Fasting helps Muslims develop self-discipline, patience and empathy for those in need. At sunset, the fast is broken with a meal called iftar, often starting with dates and water, followed by a larger meal. Many mosques offer iftar to the community, making it a time of shared experience and generosity.

Ramadan ends with Eid al-Fitr, the 'Festival of Breaking the

Fast'. This also begins with the sighting of the new moon and is a time of joy, celebration and giving. People wear new clothes, visit friends and family, and give to charity.

In the UK, with over 3 million Muslims, Ramadan is widely observed. Many schools and workplaces are aware of its importance and offer support. Fasting students might be given quiet spaces to rest or to pray, and schools may adjust PE activities. The moon, in this context, is not just a time-keeper – it signals a whole month of spiritual focus.

Passover and the Jewish calendar

The Jewish calendar follows both the moon and the sun. Each month starts with the new moon, but extra days or even whole months are added from time to time to keep the calendar in line with the seasons. This is important because many Jewish festivals are seasonal. For example, Passover must take place in spring.

Passover, or Pesach, begins on the 15th of Nisan – a date that always falls on or close to a full moon. The full moon has long been seen as a symbol of completeness and light. In Jewish tradition, it adds a sense of brightness and celebration to the start of this important holiday.

Passover commemorates the story of the Exodus, when Moses led the Israelites out of slavery in Egypt. It is a story of freedom, faith and courage. Jewish families mark the occasion with a special meal called a Seder, during which they read from the Haggadah, eat symbolic foods like matzah (unleavened bread), and retell the story.

Each part of the Seder has meaning. Bitter herbs remind people of suffering, salt water symbolises tears, and the matzah represents the speed of the escape – there was no time for the bread to rise. The Seder is full of questions and songs, helping everyone, especially children, to understand and remember the story.

In the UK, Passover is celebrated by Jewish communities across the country. Families often take time off school or work to prepare and attend Seders. The moon, shining bright at the start of the festival, adds to the sense of tradition and shared memory.

Easter and the Christian calendar

Unlike Christmas, which always falls on 25 December, Easter is a 'moveable feast' – its date changes each year. This is because Easter is tied to both the sun and the moon. Specifically, Easter Sunday is the first Sunday after the full moon following the spring equinox, which is usually around 21 March. This means Easter can fall as early as 22 March and as late as 25 April.

Easter is the most important festival in the Christian calendar. It celebrates the resurrection of Jesus Christ, three days after his crucifixion. The lead-up to Easter includes a period called Lent – 40 days of fasting or reflection – and Holy Week, which includes Palm Sunday, Maundy Thursday, Good Friday, and Easter Sunday.

Easter is celebrated in many ways – church services, sunrise gatherings, symbolic food like hot cross buns, and the giving of Easter eggs, which represent new life. In the UK, Easter is also marked by national holidays, meaning schools and many workplaces are closed on Good Friday and Easter Monday.

Even people who are not religious often take part in Easter traditions. But many do not realise that the date of Easter is carefully calculated using the moon. In this way, Christian life continues to follow a natural, seasonal rhythm, just as it has for centuries.

A shared rhythm of faith

Whether you fast during Ramadan, eat matzah at Passover, or enjoy an Easter egg on a spring Sunday, you are part of a long tradition of following the moon. The moon links people across different faiths, cultures and centuries. It reminds us that while beliefs may differ, the patterns of nature are something we all share.

In a busy modern world, where time is measured in screens and alarms, the moon still rises quietly, steadily, faithfully. Its phases mark moments of reflection, celebration and connection. It is both a physical object and a spiritual sign.

As *Psalm 104*:19 says, 'He made the moon to mark the seasons.' That line is a reminder that spiritual time and natural time are deeply connected. For millions of people in the UK and around the world, watching the moon is still a way of listening to something sacred.

Activity

1. What does Psalm 104:19 say about the moon, and why is it important in the context of religion?
2. How does the Islamic calendar use the moon to determine the start of Ramadan and Eid al-Fitr?
3. Why does the Jewish festival of Passover always begin around the time of a full moon?
4. Explain how the date of Easter is decided in the Christian calendar.
5. What are some of the shared ideas or symbols the moon represents across different religions?

Create a moon-phase calendar

Make a visual calendar showing the different phases of the moon for one month. Label which phases are linked to the start of Ramadan, Passover and Easter.

Why Muslims often don't celebrate Eid on the same day – even within one country

An article from The Conversation.

By Zuleyha Keskin, Associate Professor of Islamic Studies, Charles Sturt University

Eid is a special time for Muslims. There are two major Eid celebrations each year: Eid al-Fitr is celebrated at the end of Ramadan, the month of fasting, and Eid al-Adha is connected to the dates of Hajj, the annual pilgrimage to Mecca, Saudi Arabia.

Eid, which means 'festival' or 'feast' in Arabic, is a celebratory occasion for more than one billion Muslims worldwide. However, in some countries, especially multicultural ones like Australia, Muslims don't always celebrate Eid on the same day. Here's why.

Eid comes 10–12 days earlier each year

Beyond different groups celebrating on different days, the timing of Eid celebrations also shift as a whole each year. That's because Islam follows the lunar calendar, based on the moon's cycles – unlike the Gregorian calendar, which follows the sun.

As such, dates on the Islamic calendar come 10–12 days earlier each year. This means the dates of both Eids also move about 11 days forward each year.

In terms of the Islamic calendar:

- Eid al-Fitr happens on the 1st of the month of Shawwal (the 10th month), which comes right after the month of Ramadan.
- Eid al-Adha happens on the 10th of Dhul-Hijjah (the 12th month), during Hajj.

What about local discrepancies?

Since Islam follows the lunar calendar, determining the start of each Islamic month, and the dates of both Eids, requires sighting the new crescent moon, which comes directly after the new moon (the phase in which the moon is invisible).

But there are different methods for doing this, and different scholarly interpretations regarding what method is best. These variations are the reason one group in a community might celebrate on a Sunday, while others may celebrate on a Monday.

This means if the new crescent moon is visible in neighbouring countries, but not in Australia (such as if it's hidden behind clouds), then Australia should celebrate a

day after its neighbours. The organisation Moonsighting Australia follows this method, only declaring Eid when the moon is seen locally.

However, others argue if the moon has been sighted anywhere in the world, it should be accepted by all Muslims as the start of the new Islamic month. Some Muslims in Australia opt for this 'global moon sighting' approach, following Saudi Arabia's Eid announcement even when the moon is not sighted locally.

As far back as the early centuries AD, people in the Arab world used astrolabes to survey the skies. This instrument belonged to Yemeni sultan, mathematician and astronomer Al-Ashraf Umar II (circa 1242–1296). Metropolitan Museum of Art

Apart from the question of where the crescent moon is sighted, there are also different views over how it should be sighted. Many scholars believe in physically sighting it with the eyes, as was practised during the time of Prophet Muhammad.

But some Muslim countries, such as in Turkey and parts of Europe, use astronomical calculations to predict the new moon's birth. This allows them to pre-set the date of Eid months, or even years, in advance.

Australia versus majority-Muslim countries

In Muslim-majority countries, deciding the day of Eid happens at a government level.

For example, in Saudi Arabia, the Supreme Court officially declares the date based on moon sighting reports. This decision sets the timing for Eid prayers and public holidays for the entire nation, allowing for unified celebrations across the country.

But Muslims in Australia come from diverse cultural backgrounds, and hold varying views regarding how the moon should be sighted. Some may follow the Eid announcement from their country of origin. Others may rely on local announcements, or on dates set by peak bodies such as the Australian National Imams Council.

One 2023 report published by the ISRA Academy surveyed more than 5,500 Muslims in Australia to understand how they determined the date of Eid.

The findings reveal notable differences across communities. Respondents from the Arab community were almost evenly split between following their local mosque (28.5%) and the Australian National Imams Council (28.0%), with a slightly lower percentage (23.9%) following Moonsighting Australia. Only 0.6% followed their country of origin.

Among the Turkish community, 16.1% followed their country of origin, while the largest proportion (28.5%) relied on a local mosque or Islamic organisation. But given Turkish mosques tend to follow Turkey's state religious institution, Diyanet, most Australian Turks (44.6%) ultimately align with Turkey's decision on Eid.

Of the others, 18.8% followed Moonsighting Australia and 14.6% following the national imams' council.

In the African Muslim community, 48.4% followed Moonsighting Australia, while 32.8% relied on a local mosque, and 11.7% on the imams' council.

Eid celebrations will keep evolving

While celebrating Eid on different days may seem divisive and fragmenting, there are positive aspects to this.

For one thing, it means Australian Muslims actively seek out information from various religious authorities. This reflects a high level of public engagement in religious decisions – rather than following blindly.

The strong influence of organisations such as the Australian National Imams Council and Moonsighting Australia also suggests local religious institutions are a trusted source for guidance.

Moreover, the high percentage of Muslims now following Moonsighting Australia indicates a trend towards a localised determination of Eid. And this trend will likely become stronger with the emergence of third- and fourth-generation Australian Muslims who are less connected with their ancestral homelands.

Only time will tell whether most Australian Muslims will eventually celebrate Eid on the same day. In the meantime, families and communities continue to navigate these differences with understanding and respect.

27 March 2025

Sacred texts of major world religions

By Cory Price

The mystical pillars of all world faiths are surprisingly within reach in the form of a bundle of texts and ancient records that have been delicately protected for thousands of years. Between major world religions like Christianity, Islam, Hinduism, Buddhism, Judaism, and Taoism, monks from long-forgotten ages worked diligently to ensure the versions we carry today. Their hope was to maintain these texts to accurately represent the histories and faiths of cultures and civilisations that now exist only in their modern-day descendants.

However, many religions suffer from an occasional fracturing over core values, and with that, new sacred texts blossom in an attempt to guide the spiritual flock of that era. Furthermore, what we read today, in modern tongues, can never accurately represent the forgotten cultural references and idioms that some of these texts relied on for a specific audience. Some degree of critical analysis is necessary to approach these religious epics where some stories could have been either allegories or even stageplays that are now, possibly mistakenly, taken literally. Due to the thousands of years of historical and religious knowledge needed to decipher each of these texts, an appropriate way to begin is to ask who, what, when, where, and why? That caution is vital when considering that different faiths might revere a single religious book. Therefore, read closely to uncover the secrets and dramatic events that ultimately defined each of these sets Sacred Texts.

The world's largest religions

By studying the 10 largest ongoing faiths, one glimpses into an ancient history involving forefathers who gambled their souls on what they believed.

The Holy Bible - Christianity

Primarily, the sacred texts of Christianity are the *Old* and *New Testaments* found within the *Bible*. The *Bible* is divided into the *Old Testament*, also known as the *Torah* to the Jews, which is sacred to both Jews and Christians, and the *New Testament*, which is specifically Christian. Protestant, Orthodox, and Catholic Christians all share these texts but may have some differences in their canon. The *New Testament* is specifically centred around the teachings of Jesus Christ, whom Christians regard as God on Earth.

The *Old Testament*, also known as the Hebrew *Bible*, contains 39 books. In the Protestant *Bible*, 46 books in the Catholic *Bible*, and up to 49 books in the Orthodox *Bible*. It was written approximately between 1400 BCE and 165 BCE by multiple authors. The *New Testament* contains 27 books, which are the same across all Christian denominations. These books were written by various authors between 50 and 100 CE. The original language of the *Old Testament* is primarily Hebrew, with some portions in Aramaic, while the *New Testament* was written in (Koine) Greek.

Translations of the *Bible* have changed the original texts over time, though efforts have been made to maintain the accuracy and integrity of the translations. Language differences, cultural context, and the need for interpretation have led to variations among translations. It is also important to note that the original texts themselves have undergone changes over time due to scribal errors, editing, and additions.

Catholics have a set of books known as the *Apocrypha* or *Deuterocanonical* books, which are included in the Catholic *Old Testament* but are not accepted by most Protestants. While some Protestant denominations may refer to or study these texts for historical or cultural context, they generally do not consider them canonical or divinely inspired. Orthodox Christians also have additional texts that are not recognised by Catholics or Protestants.

The authors of the biblical texts include various prophets, apostles, and other figures throughout ancient Israel's history and the early Christian church. The study of early church tradition is especially important in Eastern Orthodoxy. The

exact authorship of many books is debated or unknown, and some books may have multiple authors or have been edited over time.

The texts within the *Bible* discuss various topics, such as the history of the Israelites, the life and teachings of Jesus Christ, ethical and moral teachings, and prophetic messages. The *Old Testament* primarily focuses on the covenant between God and the Israelites, while the *New Testament* emphasises the life, death, and resurrection of Jesus Christ and the establishment of the Christian church.

The *Quran*, *Hadith*, and The *Tafsir* - Islam

The sacred texts and written collections of Islam include the *Quran*, the *Hadith*, and the *Tafsir*. The *Quran* is the primary religious text of Islam, believed to be the literal word of God as revealed to the Prophet Muhammad by the angel Gabriel. The *Hadith* are collections of reports documenting the sayings, actions, and opinions of the Prophet Muhammad. *Tafsir* is the exegesis or interpretation of the *Quran*. There are some differences in the compilations of the *Hadith* and interpretation of the texts between Sunni and Shia Islam.

The *Quran* discusses a wide range of topics, including theology, morality, law, guidance for personal conduct, and the relationship between God and humanity. It is divided into 114 chapters called Surahs, which vary in length and cover diverse subjects. The *Hadith* collections contain reports on various aspects of the Prophet Muhammad's life, providing context and elaboration on the teachings of the *Quran*.

The *Quran* was revealed to the Prophet Muhammad over a period of 23 years (610-632 CE). The original language of the *Quran* is classical Arabic. The *Hadith* was compiled by various scholars in the first few centuries after the Prophet's death. There have been many translations of the *Quran* and *Hadith* into different languages over time, and while the translations may have varied, the original Arabic text is considered immutable.

While the *Quran* is believed to have been verbally revealed by God to the Prophet Muhammad through the angel Gabriel, the *Hadith* is slightly different. The *Hadith* was written by various scholars who collected reports from people who had direct or indirect contact with the Prophet. The most widely accepted *Hadith* collections in Sunni Islam are *Sahih al-Bukhari* and *Sahih Muslim*, while in Shia Islam, the main collections are *Al-Kafi, Man La Yahduruhu Al-Faqih, Tahdhib Al-Ahkam*, and *Al-Istibsar*.

Sunni and Shia Muslims do refer to some of each other's sacred texts, although the degree of acceptance and interpretation of the texts can differ significantly. While both Sunni and Shia Muslims accept the *Quran* as the central sacred text, they differ in their acceptance of certain *Hadith* collections. Sunni Muslims generally do not give the same

weight to Shia *Hadith* collections and vice versa. However, some common ground can be found in the study and interpretation of shared texts.

The Sacred Texts Of Hinduism

Hinduism has a vast collection of sacred texts and written collections, including the *Vedas*, *Upanishads*, *Puranas*, and more. The *Vedas* are the oldest and most important texts, composed between 1500 and 500 BCE. They consist of four parts: Rigveda, Yajurveda, Samaveda, and Atharvaveda. These texts contain hymns, mantras, rituals, and philosophical discussions. The *Upanishads* discuss the essence of reality, self, and the universe. Scribes compiled them between 800 and 500 BCE.

The *Puranas*, composed between 500 CE and 1000 CE, are a genre of religious texts that narrate the universe's history, legends, and myths. The *Bhagavad Gita*, a part of the Indian epic *Mahabharata*, is another important Hindu scripture that presents a conversation between Prince Arjuna and the God Krishna on various topics such as duty, action, and devotion.

The authors of these texts are largely unknown, though some are likely sages such as Vyasa and Valmiki. They wrote in Sanskrit, an ancient Indian language. Over time, scribes translated the texts into various languages, which could have led to differences in interpretation. However, the core teachings have largely remained consistent.

The major sects of Hinduism, such as Vaishnavism, Shaivism, Shaktism, and Smartism, acknowledge each other's sacred texts. They have different emphases and interpretations of the texts but generally accept their authority. Vaishnavism focuses on the worship of Vishnu, Shaivism on Shiva, Shaktism on the Divine Mother, and Smartism on the worship of multiple deities. Despite their differences, these sects share a common foundation in the *Vedas* and other sacred texts.

The Sacred Texts of Buddhism

Buddhism has various sacred texts, the most important of which are the *Tripitaka* and the *Mahayana Sutras*. The *Tripitaka* is the primary holy text for Theravada Buddhists, while Mahayana Buddhists revere the *Mahayana Sutras*.

The *Tripitaka*, or "Three Baskets," is a collection of three sections: the Vinaya Pitaka (monastic rules), the Sutta Pitaka (teachings and discourses), and the Abhidhamma Pitaka (philosophical and psychological analysis). The *Mahayana Sutras* encompass a vast range of texts, including the *Prajnaparamita Sutras* (Perfection of Wisdom), the *Lotus Sutra*, the *Avatamsaka Sutra*, the *Pure Land Sutras*, and the *Vimalakirti Sutra*, among others. There are also other texts in the Vajrayana tradition, such as the *Tibetan Book of the Dead*, which Vajrayana Buddhists revere.

Major Buddhist sects, such as Theravada and Mahayana, generally respect and study each other's sacred texts to some extent, recognising their shared roots and the value of diverse perspectives. However, they may prioritise their own core texts and interpret them differently according to their respective traditions and beliefs.

The sacred texts of Buddhism discuss a wide range of topics, including the teachings of the Buddha, ethical conduct, meditation, the nature of reality, the path to enlightenment, and the nature of suffering and its cessation. They also guide monastic life and the community of practitioners.

The texts' age varies, but scribes wrote down most of the *Tripitaka* between the 1st century BCE and the 1st century CE. However, the oral tradition potentially dates back to the time of the historical Buddha in the 5th century BCE. Likewise, the *Mahayana Sutras* were composed between the 1st century BCE and the 5th century CE. The original language of the *Tripitaka* is Pali, an ancient Indian language closely related to Sanskrit. The *Mahayana Sutras* were written in various languages, including Sanskrit and Gandhari.

According to traditional history, the teachings in the *Tripitaka* were transmitted orally by the disciples of the Buddha and later written down by the monastic community. The authorship of the *Mahayana Sutras* is more complex, as some texts claim to be the direct teachings of the Buddha. In contrast, others were sayings of various Buddhist masters or celestial beings. Translations of Buddhist texts have indeed changed over time, as they have been translated into numerous languages and adapted for different cultures.

The *Tanakh* And The *Talmud* - Judaism

The sacred texts of Judaism primarily include the Hebrew *Bible*, also known as the *Tanakh*, and the *Talmud*. The *Tanakh* consists of three parts: the *Torah* (Pentateuch), the *Nevi'im* (Prophets), and the *Ketuvim* (Writings). The *Talmud* is a gathering of rabbinic discussions, interpretations, and laws, which has two main versions: the Babylonian *Talmud* and the Jerusalem *Talmud*.

Different Jewish sects, such as Orthodox, Conservative, Reform, and Reconstructionist, generally accept the same sacred texts, although they may interpret them differently. All sects recognise the importance of the *Tanakh*, while the *Talmud* is primarily a central text in Orthodox and Conservative Judaism. In some cases, specific mystical or philosophical texts, such as the *Zohar*, are more prominent within particular movements, like Kabbalah and Hasidic Judaism.

Major Jewish sects generally respect each other's sacred texts, but the degree to which they use and rely on them may vary. For example, while Orthodox Judaism strictly adheres to the interpretations in the *Talmud*, Reform Judaism may not emphasise the *Talmud*'s legal aspects as much.

The sacred texts discuss a wide range of topics, from religious laws, ethics, and moral teachings to historical narratives, poetry, and prophetic visions. The *Torah* contains the foundational laws and narratives of Judaism, the *Nevi'im* recounts the stories of prophets and their messages, and the *Ketuvim* includes poetic, philosophical, and historical writings.

The Hebrew *Bible* (*Tanakh*) writings were composed over approximately 1,000 years, from the 12th to the 2nd century BCE. The language is Biblical Hebrew, with some portions in Biblical Aramaic. Scribes compiled the *Talmud* between

the 3rd and 6th centuries CE, with the Babylonian *Talmud* finishing around 500 CE and the Jerusalem *Talmud* around 400 CE. Both versions of the *Talmud* were written in a mixture of Hebrew and Aramaic.

Over time, translations of Jewish texts have evolved, and some meanings may have shifted or been lost. The *Septuagint*, a Greek translation of the Hebrew *Bible* completed in the 3rd to 2nd centuries BCE, is one of the earliest translations. Additionally, the Masoretic Text, a standardised version of the Hebrew *Bible*, was developed by Jewish scholars between the 7th and 10th centuries CE to ensure consistency in transmission and interpretation. Many modern translations are based on the Masoretic Text.

The authors of the Hebrew *Bible* were various prophets, scribes, and poets, with some parts traditionally ascribed to specific figures, like Moses for the *Torah* or King David for the *Psalms*. However, modern scholarly consensus suggests that multiple authors likely composed and edited the texts over time. The *Talmud* is a compilation of discussions by rabbis and scholars who contributed to its development over several centuries.

The Sacred Texts Of Taoism

Taoism is an ancient Chinese philosophy and religious tradition that emphasises living in harmony with the Tao, the natural flow of the universe. Its sacred texts and collections of writings are numerous and varied, reflecting the diversity of Taoist thought and practice. Significant texts include the *Tao Te Ching*, the *Zhuangzi*, and the *Daozang*. Different sects may refer to alternate collections, but these works are generally considered foundational for Taoism. Classical Chinese is the language of the original Tao texts; over time, numerous languages received their translations.

The *Tao Te Ching* is the primary text of Taoism, attributed to the legendary sage Lao Tzu. Ancient scholars recorded the oral teachings in written form around the 5th century BCE, and it consists of 81 short chapters. The text is written in Classical Chinese, discussing the nature of the Tao, the art of governing, and the principles of leading a harmonious and virtuous life.

The *Zhuangzi*, attributed to the philosopher Zhuang Zhou who wrote it around the 5th to 3rd century BCE, is another critical Taoist text. The text contains allegories, anecdotes, and parables, delving into philosophy, the relativity of human values, and the importance of spontaneous and natural living.

The *Daozang*, also known as the *Taoist Canon*, is a large collection of writings with over 1,400 texts. Emperors and dynasties compiled it in various stages between the 5th and 15th centuries. The *Daozang* contains various materials, such as scriptures, commentaries, liturgical texts, and works on alchemy, cosmology, and meditation. The content of the *Daozang* varies between different editions, reflecting the various sects and schools of Taoism.

The strength of our shared humanity has always rested on our ability to communicate with each other. That communication includes sharing practical ideas and spiritual values that guide our communities and provide hope during overwhelming distress. Each sacred text embodies that criteria: certain proverbs share information like the ideal way to harvest crops, and others teach ways to live peacefully during famine or wartime. Despite a global trend towards secularism, modern institutions are founded on many of the values that our ancestors weaved into these holy books and teachings; for that, we salute them.

15 May 2023

In spite of their differences, Jews, Christians and Muslims worship the same God

An article from The Conversation.

By Philip C. Almond, Emeritus Professor in the History of Religious Thought, The University of Queensland

It is often assumed that the God of Islam is a fierce warlike deity, in contrast to the God of Christianity and Judaism, who is one of love and mercy. And yet, despite the manifest differences in how they practise their religions, Jews, Christians and Muslims all worship the same God.

The founder of Islam, Muhammad, saw himself as the last in a line of prophets that reached back through Jesus to Moses, beyond him to Abraham and as far back as Noah. According to the *Quran*, God (known as Allah) revealed to Muhammad:

> the Book with the truth [the *Quran*], confirming what was before it, and [before He sent down the *Quran*] He sent down the *Torah* of Moses and the Gospel of Jesus... as a guidance for the people.

Thus, since Muhammad inherited the Jewish and Christian understandings of God, it is not surprising that the God of Muhammad, Jesus and Moses has a similarly complex and ambivalent character – a blend of benevolence and compassion, combined with wrath and anger. If you were obedient to his commands, he could be all sweetness and light. But you didn't want to get on his wrong side.

To those who turned to him in repentance, this God was (above all else) merciful and all-forgiving. But those who failed to find the path or, having found it failed to follow it, would know his judgment and wrath.

For Jews, God was fully revealed in the *Torah* (the first five books of the *Old Testament*). The God of the *Old Testament* was both good and evil. He went way beyond the good when he told Abraham to offer his son to God as a burnt sacrifice. He was a warrior God who murdered the firstborn of Egypt and drowned the army of Pharaoh. He approved Elijah's slaughter of the 450 prophets of the ancient Canaanite God Baal.

Yet he was also a compassionate and loving God, one who in the well-known words of *Psalm 23* in the *Book of Psalms* was a shepherd whose goodness and mercy supported his followers all the days of their lives. He loved Israel like a father loves his son.

The God of Jesus in the four Gospels in the *New Testament* had a similarly ambiguous character. On the one hand, Jesus spoke of a personal God, referring to him as "Father" in the prayer that he gave to his disciples. Yet, behind this God of tenderness and love, there remained a ruthless God of justice.

Like the prophets of the *Old Testament*, Jesus preached doom and gloom. He was offering Israel its last chance and God would be merciless to those who failed to heed his message. God would come in judgment at the end of history. All would then be resurrected. The fortunate few would receive eternal happiness, but the wicked majority would be cast into the eternal fires of hell.

So too, with the God of Muhammad. At the end of the world, God would act as a God of justice. All the dead would be resurrected to receive God's judgment. God would then reward or punish each person in the gardens of paradise or the fires of hell according to their deeds. Each would be presented with a record of his deeds – in the right hand for those to be saved, in the left for those to be damned to the fires of hell.

For those who were saved, the delights of paradise awaited. Those who died in the cause of Allah, however, did not need to wait for the Last Judgment. They would go straight to heaven.

The key to salvation was above all surrender ('islam' in Arabic) to God, obedience to his commands as revealed in the *Quran* and allegiance to his messenger Muhammad. Like the God of Moses, Allah was a lawmaker. The *Quran* provided (often varied) guidance to the believing community in matters of marriage and family law, women, inheritance, food and drink, worship and purity, warfare, punishments for adultery and false accusations of adultery, alcohol and theft. In short, it provided the foundation of what was later to be much elaborated in sharia law.

Muslims, Christians and Jews do all worship the same complex God. Yet, in spite of this, all believe that their religion contains the full and final revelation of the same God. Here is the origin of their unity. Here also lies the cause of their division.

For this belief in the truth of one religion and the falsity of the others leads to inevitable conflict between the believer and the unbeliever, the chosen and the rejected, the saved and the damned. Here lie the seeds of intolerance and violence.

So the God of Muhammad, like the God of Jesus and Moses, divides as much as he unites, a cause of strife both between and within these religions.

6 September 2017

Religion in the UK today

Religion in the UK today is a complex and diverse subject. While the country has deep Christian roots, especially through the Church of England, recent decades have seen a significant shift in religious identity. Fewer people now identify as religious, but those who do are often more committed to their beliefs. At the same time, the UK has become home to a wide variety of faiths, reflecting a more multicultural society.

According to the 2021 Census, less than half the population of England and Wales now identify as Christian (46.2%) – the first time this has happened. In 2001, nearly three-quarters of people described themselves as Christian. Over the same period, the number of people saying they have 'no religion' has grown rapidly, with more than a third of the population now ticking that box. This suggests that Britain is becoming more secular, especially among younger generations who are less likely to be raised with religious traditions.

However, this does not mean that religion is disappearing from British life. For many people, religious identity remains important, both personally and as part of their community. The number of people identifying as Muslim has increased, making Islam the second largest religion in the UK. There are also growing numbers of people following Hinduism, Sikhism, Buddhism, and Judaism. These communities often have strong family ties, shared traditions, and places of worship that act as centres of support and celebration.

Religious festivals are widely recognised across the UK, with holidays such as Christmas, Easter, Diwali, Eid, and Hanukkah celebrated by different groups. Schools and workplaces are increasingly aware of the importance of respecting religious practices, such as prayer times, dietary rules, and religious dress. In politics, too, there is greater awareness of religious diversity, although some challenges remain around inclusion and discrimination.

Faith also plays a visible role in charity and community work. Many religious organisations provide support for people in need, whether through food banks, homeless shelters, or refugee support. Religious values often inspire acts of kindness, compassion, and justice, and many people are drawn to religion for a sense of purpose or belonging.

At the same time, religion in the UK faces challenges. Some people feel that religion is outdated or out of touch with modern values, especially around topics like gender and sexuality. Others are concerned about the rise of religious extremism, which can lead to suspicion or misunderstanding. There are also debates about the role of religion in public life, including whether the Church of England should continue to have special status as the established church.

Overall, religion in the UK today is marked by contrast. On one hand, there is a growing number of people who do not follow a religion. On the other, those who do are often part of rich, diverse, and vibrant communities. As the UK continues to change, religion remains an important part of many people's lives – offering comfort, tradition, identity, and a sense of belonging in an often confusing world.

Does the UK protect our Right To Freedom of Religion or Belief?

By Khadija Kothia, Aziz Foundation Intern Journalist

In 1975, at the height of Cold War tensions, leaders of the United States, Canada and all European countries sat down together in Helsinki, Finland. Their main aim was to discuss how to improve relations between different factions of the world when a global armed conflict felt dangerously close.

Together, they agreed upon the right to freedom of thought, conscience, religion or belief. These agreements – along with many other rights – would contribute to the overall security and social cohesion of society.

Since 1975, the Organisation for Security and Co-operation in Europe (OSCE) has developed a programme to promote and protect the Freedom of Religion or Belief across the 57 countries of the OSCE region, including the United Kingdom.

After all these years, how much respect does the UK provide to the right to freedom of thought, conscience, religion or belief?

First off, what does the right to freedom of religion or belief entail?

- It is universal
- It is protected by international human rights law
- It cannot be suspended even during a state of emergency
- It is broadly constructed
- It has both internal and external dimensions

What does the European Convention on Human Rights (ECHR) say?

The right to freedom of religion or belief is enshrined in many binding and non-binding international human rights instruments: in Article 18 of the Universal Declaration of Human Rights, Article 18 of International Covenant on Civil and Political Rights, Article 9 of European Convention on Human Rights and many commitments of the OSCE.

Article 9 of the ECHR says:

(1) Everyone has the right to freedom of thought, conscience and religion; this right includes freedom to change his religion or belief and freedom, either alone or in community with others and in public or private, to manifest his religion or belief, in worship, teaching, practice and observance.

(2) Freedom to manifest one's religion or beliefs shall be subject only to such limitations as are prescribed by law and are necessary in a democratic society in the interests of public safety, for the protection of public order, health or morals, or for the protection of the rights and freedoms of others.

Does the UK protect our right to freedom of religion or belief?

The 1998 Human Rights Act protects freedom of thought, conscience and religion, and reaffirms Article Nine of the European Convention of Human Rights (see above), subject to certain restrictions that are 'in accordance with law' and 'necessary in a democratic society'. By incorporating the right to freedom of religion or belief into UK law, British citizens can go to a court to have this right protected by a judge.

In 2018–2019, the government recorded a 3% increase (up to 8,566 offences) in religiously motivated hate crimes in England and Wales. This included 1,805 anti-semitic incidents during the year, the highest recorded by the Community Security Trust (CST), up 7% from the preceding year. This increase includes assaults, extreme violence, non-violent abusive behaviour and online incidents.

There was also an increase in the number of anti-Muslim hate incidents in 2018, which showed 3,173 reports, the highest number since the NGO Tell MAMA's founding in 2011. A European Commission (EC) survey published in September showed that 61% of respondents believed discrimination based on religion or belief was very or fairly widespread in the country.

'In 2018-2019, the government recorded a 3% increase (up to 8,566 offences) in religiously motivated hate crimes in England and Wales.'

Some people blame the government and, in particular, the prime minister for rising anti-religious discrimination. Boris Johnson failed to apologise for his comments about Muslim women in a 2018 opinion article, the same year that Tell MAMA recorded its highest number of anti-Muslim attacks. In the same year, CST recorded 100 anti-semitic incidents monthly during the year. The two highest single monthly totals came in February and December, which coincided with months when the main opposition Labour Party faced allegations of anti-semitism, with CST stating that the Labour anti-Semitism controversy 'clearly has an important bearing' on the rising anti-semitic attacks.

Since then, and particularly after the Christchurch New Zealand mosque attack in 2019, the government has increased its attention towards improving protections to the right to freedom of religion or belief. The government doubled the amount of funding from £800,000 in 2018–2019 to £1.6 million from 2019–2020 to provide security at places of worship and related security training. They also created and filled two new positions dealing with religious freedom issues: an independent advisor on anti-semitism and an independent advisor appointed to provide expert advice on a definition of islamophobia, and appointed a new special envoy for freedom of religion or belief.

What about now?

Now, in 2021, the COVID-19 pandemic has increased religious discrimination across the world. Many religious minorities have been scapegoated. In Britain, some are noticing that there has also been a pattern of using irrelevant images of religious minorities, such as Muslims, in negative reports on COVID-19, which has increased fears within minority religious groups that religious minorities may be targeted in conspiracy theories about disease-ridden communities.

21 March 2021

Questions

1. What does Article 9 of the Human Rights Act protect?
2. How does the UK law define the right to freedom of religion or belief?
3. Can the right to manifest religion or belief be restricted under UK law? If so, under what conditions?
4. What are some examples given in the article of how religious freedom has been protected in the UK courts?
5. Why might some people feel that their freedom of religion is not fully respected in the UK?
6. How have UK schools been involved in debates about religious expression?
7. What role does the Equality Act 2010 play in protecting religious freedom?
8. How does the law treat situations where religious rights come into conflict with other rights?
9. What are the limits of religious freedom when it comes to harming others or breaking the law?
10. Why is it important to balance individual rights with the rights and freedoms of others in a diverse society?

The above information is reprinted with kind permission from EachOther.

www.eachother.org.uk

How religious are British people?

A quarter of Britons say they believe in 'a god'. Four in ten neither believe in 'a god' nor in a 'higher power'.

By Milan Dinic

Although the United Kingdom is a monarchy formally led by a ruler who also governs the official church – the Church of England – belief in 'a god' in the UK is low. Only a quarter of Britons (27%) say they actually believe in 'a god'. A further one in six (16%) believe in the existence of 'a higher spiritual power', but not 'a god'.

Amongst British Christians, just over half (56%) believe in the existence of God, whilst 16% believe in a higher power. One in ten (10%) of British Christians say they do not believe there is 'a god' or 'a higher power'.

Belief in 'a god' is low across all age groups. Older Britons – those aged 60 and above – are the most likely to believe in a supreme deity, but even there just a third (36%) hold this view.

Overall, four in ten (41%) Britons believe there is neither 'a god' nor 'a higher power'. Younger generations are the most likely to think there is no greater force out there, including 50% of 25-39 year olds and 45% of 16-24 year olds, compared to 32% of those 60 and over.

About two in five Britons believe in a god or a higher power

Do you believe in a god or a higher spiritual power? %

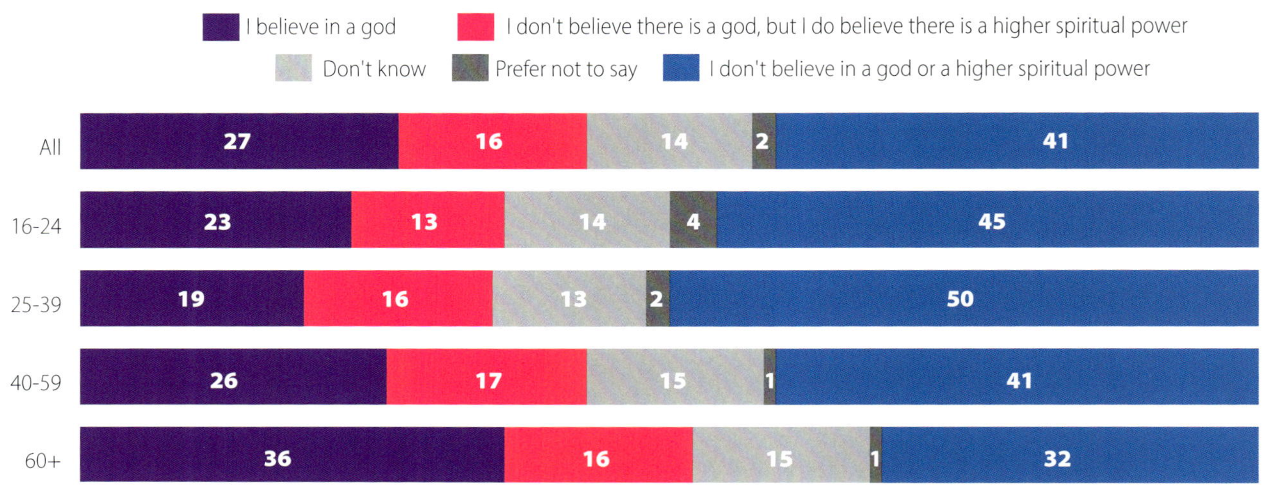

Source: YouGov

Most Britons say they are not religious

Do you regard yourself as belonging to any particular religion, and if so, to which of these do you belong? %

Women (48%) are notably more likely than men (36%) to say they believe in the existence of 'a god'/'a higher spiritual power'. A quarter (28%) of women believe there is 'a god', whilst one in five (20%) believe that there is some form of a higher spiritual power.

Religiousness in Britain

Over half (55%) of Britons say they do not belong to any particular religion. A third (35%) belong to one of the recognised Christian denominations (20% to the Church of England and the rest to other denominations). A further 7% belong to other religions.

A quarter of religious people (23%) said their religion is 'very important' to them, and a further third (32%) say it is 'somewhat important'. However, four in ten (42%) of those who belong to a particular religion say it doesn't play an important role in their lives.

The gender breakdown of the results shows that more women (59%) than men (51%) consider religion to be important in their lives.

Amongst British Christians, 44% say that religion isn't important in their life. Only half as many (22%) of those who belong to other religions say the same.

29 December 2020

Over two in five British Christians say religion is not important in their life

How important is religion in your life? % of 760 Christians

Source: YouGov

The above information is reprinted with kind permission from YouGov.

www.yougov.co.uk

God, heaven and hell, and life after death: data reveals UK's low religious belief compared with other nations

The share of the British public who identify as religious has halved since the 1980s.

The UK public are now among the least likely internationally to believe in God, following a long-term decline in belief since the 1980s, according to a new study.

The research, led by the Policy Institute at King's College London, also finds that the share of the population who say God is not important in their life is at a record high, having doubled compared with four decades ago.

Belief in heaven has decreased over the same period, but belief in life after death and hell has remained stable, with younger generations more inclined to believe in both – despite being less religious generally.

At the same time, the proportion of Britons who consider themselves religious has nearly halved, and out of 24 countries included in the research, only four are less likely to identify as religious than the UK.

But while the country is becoming less religious, the UK is second only to Sweden for trust in people of different faiths, and has high religious tolerance as well as increasing confidence in churches and religious organisations.

The analysis was carried out as part of the World Values Survey (WVS), one of the largest and most widely used academic social surveys in the world, in operation since 1981.

The latest UK data was collected in 2022, with data for other nations collected at various points throughout the latest wave of the WVS, which spanned 2017 to 2022.

Belief in God, heaven, hell and life after death

God

Just under half (49%) of Britons said they believed in God in 2022 – down from three-quarters (75%) in 1981.

Of 24 nations in the study, only five are now less likely than the UK to say they believe in God, with China (17%) by far the least likely to.

And the share of the British public who say God is not important in their life has doubled and is now at a record high, rising from 28% to 57% between 1981 and 2022.

Just five out of 24 countries are less likely than the UK (23%) to say God is important to them, including Japan (14%), Sweden (14%) and China (8%).

Heaven and hell

Between 1981 and 2022, the share of the public believing in heaven fell from 57% to 41%.

Despite this, the idea of heaven is still more popular than hell, which 26% said they believed in in 2022 – a figure largely unchanged since trends began.

While younger people have lower levels of religious belief and are more likely to identify as atheists, Gen Z (32%) and Millennials (32%) are in fact more likely than Baby Boomers (18%) and the pre-war generation (24%) to believe in hell.

And by international standards, the UK is less likely to believe in hell, ranking 17th out of 24 countries – and far behind some peer nations such as the US (69%) and Italy (39%).

Life after death

Views on life after death have held up well over the last four decades, with just under half of the public – including 46% in 2022 – consistently saying they believe in it.

And again, despite their lack of faith, younger people have higher levels of belief: in 2022, majorities of Gen Z (51%) and Millennials (53%) said they believed in life after death – higher than the share of Baby Boomers (35%) and the pre-war generation (39%) who said the same.

The UK public are among the least likely internationally to identify as religious

In 1981, 57% of Britons considered themselves religious. By 2022, this had nearly halved, falling to 32%.

Over the same period, the proportion who see themselves as atheists has increased fivefold, from 4% to 21%, with a notable uptick between 2018 and 2022.

And of 24 major countries analysed:

- Only those in Sweden (27%), South Korea (16%), China (16%) and Japan (14%) are less likely than people in the UK to consider themselves religious.
- Just four – Australia (30%), Sweden (28%), Japan (15%) and China (13%) – rank below the UK (31%) for saying religion is important in their life.
- The UK is very tolerant of different faiths despite not being very religious.
- 82% of the UK public say they trust people of a different religion – the second highest of 24 nations, behind only Sweden (87%) and on a par with Norway (82%).
- And among a smaller sample of 17 countries where the question was asked, only Germany (10%) and Japan (11%) are less likely than people in the UK (12%) to agree that the only acceptable religion is their religion.
- This compares with 90% of people in Morocco, at the other end of the table, who hold this view.
- And confidence in religious institutions has begun to rebound.
- Between 1981 and 2018, Britons' confidence in churches and religious organisations fell from 49% to 31%, but by 2022 had risen again, to 42%.
- However, of 24 countries, the UK still ranks among the bottom half for confidence in such institutions, including behind the likes of Norway (50%), Italy (53%) and the US (54%).

David Voas, professor of social science at UCL, said:

'The findings point to both the long-established erosion of religious involvement and to some interesting complexity in our self-perception and who believes what. The main story remains that most people in Britain aren't very interested in religion. That said, the glass remains half full when it comes to belief in God or life after death. Adults under 40 are much more likely than older people to call themselves atheists, but also to say that they believe in hell, which is a fascinating puzzle.

'While the British seem comfortable with their widely shared lack of religiosity, they have little objection to others being different, at least so long as religion doesn't intrude into public affairs. The survey even shows an unexpected uptick in confidence in churches and religious organisations.'

Bobby Duffy, professor of public policy and director of the Policy Institute at King's College London, said:

'Our cultural attachment to organised religion has continued to decline in the UK – but our belief that there is something beyond this life is holding strong, including among the youngest generations. This reflects a long-term pattern, where those who feel actively connected to organised religions have moved from a "conscript" army in previous decades, where many more felt it was an automatic part of life, to a more 'professional' army, which are fewer in number but more dedicated in practice.

'This is an important period in the development of religiosity and spirituality in western countries like the UK, where the findings show that while the youngest generations continue to have lower attachment to formal religion, many of them have similar or even greater need to believe that there is 'more than this'.

'And of course, these sorts of international studies show that the decline of organised religion is not really a global story at all – as it continues to grow and flourish in many countries around the world, and these changes are really constrained to countries like the UK.'

19 May 2023

Gen Z far less likely to be atheists than parents and grandparents, new study reveals

With many of younger generation found to identify as 'spiritual', research counters assumption spirituality is on decline and in fact implies God is 'making a comeback'.

By Tara Cobham

Gen Z's in their teens or in their twenties are far less likely to be atheists than their parents and grandparents, with many more identifying as 'spiritual', a new study has revealed.

The research counters assumptions that spirituality is on the decline and in fact implies God is 'making a comeback', with the younger generation the least likely to call themselves atheists, while middle-aged Generation X proving the most.

The survey of 10,000 people found only 13% of under 25s identified as atheists, whereas 62% of 18- to 24-year-olds said they are 'very' or 'fairly' spiritual.

Comparatively, the poll conducted by OnePoll showed as many as a quarter of those aged between 45 and 60 called themselves an atheist.

Then, 20% of those in both the Baby Boomer generation, over 65s, and Millennials aged between 25 to 44 described themselves as atheists.

But only 35 per cent of Baby Boomers, 36 per cent of 55 to 64 year olds, and 52 per cent of millennials aged between 35 to 44 said they are 'very' or 'fairly' spiritual.

Christopher Gasson, who commissioned the research, called the results 'gobsmacking' and told The Times they imply that God is 'making a comeback' in the UK.

But Mr Gasson, who is the author of *The Devil's Gospels: Finding God in Four Great Atheist Books,* did add: 'I imagine many church leaders will be rubbing their hands thinking this is the answer to their prayers but unfortunately for them, it isn't... Whatever the survey might say about young people being more spiritual and religious than old people, it is equally clear that they are put off by established religion.'

Gen Z's responses to how they 'feed' their sense of the spiritual included 'enjoying nature' and 'mindfulness', not 'participating in religious practices'.

This backs up figures from the Church of England, which show close to a third of churches have 'zero children' among their congregation.

According to a report last week, Gen Z are in fact more likely to be interested in astrology, with social media platforms such as TikTok seeing a boom in astrology-based feeds. Co-Star, an American app combining Nasa data and content from astrologers, rocketed from 7.5 million global users in 2020 to 30 million in 2023, while spending on astrology-related products is projected to grow to $22.8 billion by 2031, up from $12.8 billion in 2021.

Another explanation suggested for this trend is the religious backgrounds of the younger generation, with it being widely reported that Christian parents are often less successful at passing on their faith to their children.

Out of the 1,039 respondents aged under 25, 40% of those identified as Christian, while 21% said they are Muslim, and three% are Hindu.

Meanwhile, out of the 2,356 respondents aged over 65, as many as 69% called themselves Christian, compared to one% Muslim or Hindu.

The survey also questioned 1,696 25 to 34 year olds, 1,637 35 to 44 year olds, 1,667 45 to 54 year olds, and 1,605 55 to 64 year olds.

28 January 2025

Religion in England and Wales: what the 2021 Census tells us

The 2021 Census provides a fascinating insight into the religious make-up of England and Wales. For the first time since records began, fewer than half the population described themselves as Christian. This shift reflects a changing society where a wider range of beliefs – and non-beliefs – are openly expressed.

According to the data, 46.2% of people identified as Christian, down from 59.3% in 2011. This marks a significant decline over ten years and highlights how more people are moving away from traditional religious identities. At the same time, 37.2% of people said they had no religion – a sharp increase from 25% in the previous census. An additional 6% chose not to answer the question on religion.

Among the other main religions, Islam was the second most common, with 6.5% of the population identifying as Muslim. Hinduism accounted for 1.7%, Sikhism 0.9%, and both Judaism and Buddhism each made up 0.5%. Another 0.6% of people followed religions not listed in the main categories.

The 'other religion' group is particularly diverse and reveals a growing interest in smaller or less mainstream faiths. For instance, 74,000 people identified as Pagan, making it the largest group within this category. Other notable write-ins included Alevi (26,000), Jain (25,000), Wicca (13,000), Ravidassia (10,000), Shamanism (8,000), Rastafarian (6,000), and Zoroastrian (4,000). These figures show the rich tapestry of belief systems now present across England and Wales.

Some people used the 'Any other religion' option to write in non-religious belief systems. The largest of these were Agnostic (32,000), Atheist (14,000), and Humanist (10,000). While technically not religions, their inclusion highlights how some individuals still want to describe their worldview in a way that reflects a sense of identity or philosophy of life.

The data also shows how religion is a personal and often complex matter. For many, faith remains a core part of daily life, culture, and community. For others, religion is no longer relevant or never played a role to begin with. The increase in those identifying with no religion suggests a move towards more secular values, though it does not necessarily mean a loss of moral or spiritual belief.

Understanding the religious composition of a country is important in a multicultural society. It helps schools, councils, and government bodies better support different communities and ensure that services are inclusive. It also encourages greater awareness and respect for the wide range of beliefs people hold.

The 2021 Census paints a picture of a society that is both increasingly diverse and increasingly secular. As England and Wales continue to change, these patterns of belief and non-belief will remain an important part of our shared story.

By the time of the next census in 2031, it is likely that religion in England and Wales will continue to reflect a more diverse and secular society. The number of people identifying as Christian may decline further, while those stating they have no religion could become the largest group overall. Smaller faiths and spiritual paths – such as Paganism, Jainism, or Wicca – may continue to grow as people explore different forms of belief. At the same time, more individuals may identify with non-religious worldviews like agnosticism, atheism, or humanism. Immigration and cultural exchange could also lead to growth in religions such as Islam, Hinduism, and Sikhism. Overall, religious identity may become more fluid, with people feeling more confident in expressing both traditional and alternative beliefs – or choosing not to follow any religion at all.

Infographic

Using the data in this article, create an infographic to show the religious make up of the UK in the 2021 census.

The big idea: do we still need religion?

In a world of scientific miracles, what does faith have to offer us?

By Robin Dunbar

In 2018, archaeologists moving bodies for reburial from a 19th-century cemetery in Birmingham to make way for the new HS2 station were puzzled to find several that had plates on their laps. Then someone remembered a curious custom from the nearby Welsh Marches – that of the village 'sin-eater'. A plate of bread and salt would be placed on the deceased's lap while they were lying in repose. Just before the coffin was closed and the funeral cortege set off for the church, the village sin-eater arrived, ate the bread and was given some coins and a glass of ale for their trouble. The belief was that the deceased's sins were absorbed by the salt and transferred into the bread, and then into the sin-eater.

Sin-eaters were usually elderly and destitute, and glad to have the money – not to mention the free food and drink. The price they paid was to be shunned by their community because of their macabre associations. The last known sin-eater was Richard Munslow, who died aged 73 in 1906. Sin-eating reminds us that, more than anything else, even the most staid of religions – in this case, Anglicanism – can be associated with surprisingly curious beliefs and rituals.

Perhaps because of this, it has often been claimed that religious belief arises from ignorance and superstition. If that were the case, you might expect religion to gradually fade away as societies became better educated and more scientifically oriented.

There are at least two reasons, however, why religions persist. One is the fact that, on average, religious people are generally happier, healthier and live longer. For better or for worse, they also have easier deaths when the time comes. The other is that religious people are more likely to feel that they belong to a community. In a survey I ran, those who reported attending religious services were depressed less frequently, felt their lives were more worthwhile, were more engaged with their local community, and felt greater trust towards others. These enormous benefits mean not only that religion has enduring appeal, but that religious practices make you 'fit' in the evolutionary sense – and thus they tend to stick around.

Part of the reason people are attracted to religion is that its rituals – the standing, sitting and kneeling in unison, the singing, the listening to emotionally rousing sermons – trigger the brain's endorphin system. This is the mechanism that underpins social bonding in all primates, including humans. Like opiates, endorphins produce a sense of bliss bordering on ecstasy, calmness and warmth, relaxation and

trust, while elevating pain thresholds. In addition to these hedonic benefits, endorphins trigger the release of natural killer cells (part of the body's immune system).

Endorphins also underpin the bonding of friendships and, through that, allow us to create supportive groups of like-minded individuals. This effect seems to be especially strong in the context of rituals, as has been shown experimentally in religious services in the UK and Brazil. It seems, therefore, that religions evolved to reinforce a sense of community cohesion, something that's extremely important to our wellbeing and survival.

A penchant for religion is part of our genetic inheritance

Our natural community size – the size of our personal social network, the number of friends we have on Facebook – is part of a relationship between group size and brain size in primates. Each species has a characteristic group size determined by the size of its brain. Ours is about 150. Not only is this the average size of personal social networks (the number of extended family and friends with whom you have meaningful relationships), but it also turns out to be the optimal size for religious congregations. If a congregation is smaller than about 100, it puts a heavy burden on the membership; if it is above about 200, it becomes increasingly prone to divisiveness. This seems to explain why big religions are so susceptible to fragmentation – constantly throwing up small sects (typically of a few hundred people at most) built round a charismatic leader whose wayward beliefs the hierarchy desperately tries to contain.

Social bonding is important, of course, to many species. But there's an aspect of religion that seems to be peculiarly human. Being able to engage in religious discussion – and hence explain the significance of the rituals and why you should take part – depends on the kinds of mind-reading, or 'mentalising', skills that play a crucial role in managing our everyday relationships. These are the skills that allow us to understand what someone else is thinking, to grasp their intentions. They allow us to utter sentences such as, 'I know that you realise that Freddie believes that …'

To be able to do this, I have to be able to step back from the immediacy of the physical world so as to imagine the possibility that you might or might not think this, that Freddie might or might not intend whatever you thought he did, and even whether the person Freddie had in mind did or did not think what Freddie thought they did. Apes can do the first two steps in this chain, but that's the limit. For humans, it comes easily, bringing with it an ability to imagine parallel worlds inhabited by invisible beings. It's a short step from there to religious ideas, which in turn lead to better bonding, which makes you more likely to survive. Survival means your superior mentalising skills will be passed on to a new generation, equally adept at religious thinking; a penchant for religion is therefore part of our genetic inheritance.

But that's not all. The same cognitive abilities that give us religion also allow us to ask why the world has to be the way it is (giving us science) and to imagine entirely fictional worlds (giving us literature). Thus, you could no more have a world where religion was cast aside as superstition than you could have one without science or stories. And that would be a very different world indeed.

28 March 2022

Questions

1. Why do some people believe religion is no longer necessary in modern society?
2. What are some of the reasons given in the article for why religion might still be important today?
3. How does the article describe the role of community in religion?
4. What is meant by the idea that religion can offer a 'moral framework'?
5. Do you think religion and science can exist side by side, or are they in conflict? Why?

Debate

Split the class into two groups: one arguing that religion is still needed in modern society, and one arguing that it is not. Each group should prepare three points and present them.

Reflection

Write a short personal reflection on whether you believe religion is helpful, harmful, or a mix of both in today's world, and explain why.

Research and write

Choose one world religion and write a short paragraph about how it helps to create a sense of community for its followers.

Useful Websites

Useful websites

www.eachother.org.uk

www.cjfaderogao.blogspot.com

www.independent.co.uk

www.kcl.ac.uk

www.theconversation.com

www.theguardian.com

www.understandingreligion.org.uk

www.worldatlas.com

www.yougov.co.uk

www.yourdictionary.com

Glossary

Afterlife
Beliefs about what happens after death. Different religions have different ideas, such as heaven, rebirth, or spiritual peace.

Agnosticism
The belief that we can't know for sure whether God or gods exist. Agnostics often say, 'I don't know,' or 'It's impossible to know.'

Atheism
The belief that there is no God or gods. Atheists live without following a religion or believing in a higher power.

Blasphemy
Speaking or acting in a way that insults or disrespects something a religion sees as sacred, like God, holy books, or rituals.

Buddhism
A religion based on the teachings of Buddha, focusing on peace, meditation, and ending suffering through kindness and wisdom.

Christianity
A monotheistic religion based on the life and teachings of Jesus Christ. Christians follow the *Bible* and believe in love, forgiveness, and salvation.

Faith
A strong belief or trust in something, especially in a religion or spiritual idea, even without having physical proof.

Hinduism
One of the world's oldest religions, with many gods and goddesses. Hinduism teaches ideas like karma, reincarnation, and living in harmony.

Holy book
A text that contains a religion's teachings, stories, and rules. Examples include the *Bible*, *Qur'an*, *Torah*, and *Vedas*.

Humanism
A non-religious belief system that values reason, empathy, and human rights. Humanists believe we can be good without needing religion.

Islam
A monotheistic religion based on the teachings of the Prophet Muhammad. Muslims follow the *Qur'an* and focus on peace, prayer, and charity.

Judaism
One of the oldest monotheistic religions. Jewish people follow the *Torah* and celebrate traditions like the Sabbath and Passover.

Monotheism
The belief in one God. Religions like Christianity, Islam, and Judaism are monotheistic.

Morality
Ideas about what is right and wrong. Religions often teach morals to guide how people treat each other.

Pilgrimage
A journey to a sacred place for religious reasons – like Muslims going to Mecca or Christians visiting Lourdes.

Polytheism
The belief in many gods. Religions like Hinduism (in some traditions) and some ancient religions are polytheistic.

Prayer
Speaking to or connecting with a God or higher power, often asking for help, giving thanks, or seeking guidance.

Religion
A set of beliefs, values, and practices–often about a higher power–that help people understand life, purpose, and how to live.

Religious persecution
When people are treated unfairly, harmed, or discriminated against because of their religion or beliefs.

Religious slaughter
A way of killing animals for food that follows religious rules, such as halal in Islam or kosher in Judaism.

Ritual
A religious ceremony or action done in a set way, such as prayer, fasting, or lighting candles.

Sacred
Something considered holy or very special within a religion – like a place, object, book, or time.

Secular
Not connected to religion. A secular country or school keeps religion separate from laws, education, and public life.

Sikhism
A monotheistic religion founded in India by Guru Nanak. Sikhs believe in equality, service to others, and devotion to one God.

Spirituality
A personal sense of connection to something bigger than ourselves. It may or may not be linked to religion.

Tolerance
Respecting other people's beliefs, even if they're different from your own – an important value in diverse communities.

Worship
Showing deep respect, love, or devotion to a God or higher power – often through prayer, music, or gathering together.

Index